Wicked NIAGARA

Wicked Niagara

THE SINISTER SIDE OF THE NIAGARA FRONTIER

LORNA MACDONALD CZARNOTA

THE History PRESS

Published by The History Press
Charleston, SC 29403
www.historypress.net

First published 2011

Manufactured in the United States

ISBN 978.1.60949.227.4

Library of Congress Cataloging-in-Publication Data

Czarnota, Lorna.
Wicked Niagara / Lorna Czarnota.
p. cm.
Includes bibliographical references.
ISBN 978-1-60949-227-4
1. Crime--Niagara River Region (N.Y. and Ont.)--History--Anecdotes. 2. Crime--New York (State)--Niagara Falls Region--History--Anecdotes. 3. Corruption--Niagara River Region (N.Y. and Ont.)--History--Anecdotes. 4. Corruption--New York (State)--Niagara Falls Region--History--Anecdotes. 5. Niagara River Region (N.Y. and Ont.)--History--Anecdotes. 6. Niagara Falls Region (N.Y.)--History--Anecdotes. 7. Niagara River Region (N.Y. and Ont.)--Social conditions--Anecdotes. 8. Niagara Falls Region (N.Y.)--Social conditions--Anecdotes. 9. Niagara River Region (N.Y. and Ont.)--Moral conditions--Anecdotes. 10. Niagara Falls Region (N.Y.)--Moral conditions--Anecdotes. I. Title.
HV6793.N62C92 2011
364.109747'98--dc22
2011014953

Contents

Contents

Acknowledgements

Before I thank the people who helped with the information in this book, I wish to thank my parents, David and Mary MacDonald, who passed just months before I began writing this book. They were very proud of my first writings and the work I have accomplished over the years. I know they would have been very excited about this book also. Mom was a creative spirit, and Dad had a thirst for knowledge and was fascinated with and excited about life. Both gave me the foundation that led to this work.

Mom and Dad, you are missed everyday. Thank you for the many years of support and encouragement. I would not have done anything I am now doing had you not set the wheels in motion. I am eternally grateful.

My heartfelt thanks go out to the many historians and researchers who collected the sources used to make the stories in this book. Special thanks to Fort Niagara, United States History Images, collector David Rumsey, photographer Shaun O'Boyle and Daniel DiLandro from the *Buffalo Courier-Express* Library for your time and generosity. For more information on these kind folks, please see the bibliography.

Thank you to my editor, Whitney Tarella, for your guidance and answering my many questions; also for your enthusiasm about this project. Also, I wish to thank Jaime Muehl, senior editor, who worked not only on this book but also on my last one for The History Press, as well as the fine artists for their cover and interior book designs.

Thank you to the Buffalo Erie County Historical Society for making information about our region available to those who need it.

Last but not least, I would like to thank my significant other, Thomas, for the countless hours of listening to me tell and read the stories and for proofreading, as well as supplying dinners, space to work and understanding what it means to be an artist and author.

Introduction

The Niagara region comprises thousands of acres of rich territory along the southeastern border of Canada and the northwestern border of New York State. Named for the mighty Niagara River, this region played an important role in the formation of both countries. Wild and seemingly unstoppable, the Niagara, which takes its name from the early native people of the region, is a force to be reckoned with, tamed only for the creation of electricity and entertainment, both deadly and legendary. Perhaps the best description of its ability to incite the imagination and to carry us to the darker side of the self is an infamous vaudeville sketch, a sample of which follows.

Two strangers meet, and one greets the other: "I once was a happy man like you. I had a beautiful wife, and we were happy together. We had a nice home. I had a good job. Then one day, I came home to find my wife gone and a note saying she left with another man."

"Oh, that's terrible," acknowledges the second man.

"Pal, you don't know the half of it. I chased them all the way to Boston and then to Philadelphia, Miami and finally caught up with them in Western New York. I saw him standing there with his back to me, leaning against the railing at Niagara Falls."

The bit begins with this first man turning on the other. "So slowly I turned, step by step, inch by inch. I walked up to him and hit him in the head! I smashed his face, tore his clothes…" At this point, the first man is brutally beating the second man, the second man having been, up until now, innocently listening to the story. Moments later, the first man recovers his senses.

"Pal, oh I am so sorry," he says, brushing off the second man and backing up to the other end of the stage. "It's just, when I hear that name, it makes me crazy."

The second man replies innocently, "What name? You mean Niagara Falls?"

"Slowly I turn, step by step, inch by inch—" and the attack repeats, to hysterical laughter from the audience.

If the actors are good at their craft, the sketch never grows old, just like the Niagara Region, in all its ancient splendor, continues to spellbind the visitor.

This region was built by the native peoples but also by settlers, warfare, slavery and industry, on the backs and through the sweat of many creative and hardworking people. However, there is another story to tell. That is a story of the darker side of the rainbow that forms over the mighty river. It is the story of Wicked Niagara, one that we keep buried deep in the locked box lest someone should open it and release its evil. These are tales told in whispers.

Wealth and Power

The Struggle for Control

Native peoples settled near the waterways that gave them food, drink and transportation. Others came here, too. The French used the Niagara as a gateway to the upper Great Lakes and the Ohio and Mississippi River Valleys, claiming what they could and bypassing the English, who held the eastern coast. Later, French, British and American colonists all fought to control this corridor for western expansion. Beyond these days of war, entrepreneurs came and built. Those seeking to make their way in this country, where streets were "paved with gold," found a new welcoming home and work in the Niagara region. And as with any civilization where peoples mix and attempt to thrive, they brought with them their corruptions.

It is impossible to separate the history of the Niagara Region from its waterways. Lake Erie, Lake Ontario, the Niagara River and the Erie Canal all played a vital role in the creation of what is good and what is dark and sinister. These waterways brought not only goods but also pioneers—people who serviced the waterways or traveled by them to other regions and some who settled in the Niagara Region to build lives for their families and their businesses. Not all of those businesses were aboveboard or legal, as in the case of smuggling and organized crime. Not all of the people were shining examples of good character. Although the native peoples revered the natural environment, their story is human, and as such, it is one of survival. Even their civilization was formed from a struggle with light and dark.

The large expanse of rich land and water is not without its limits; natural resources can be overtaxed and overwhelmed by the needs of man. The

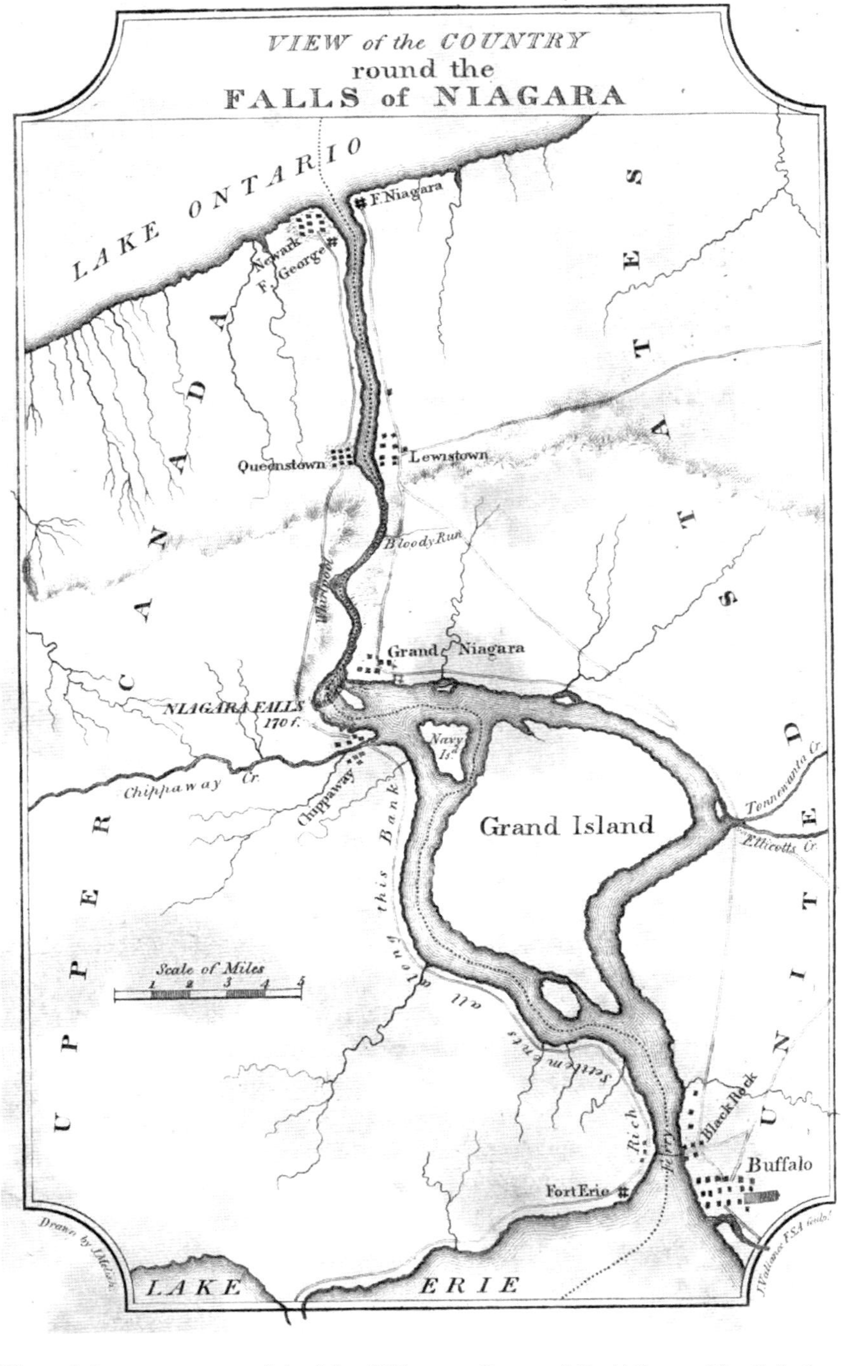

View of the country around the falls of Niagara. *Courtesy of David Rumsey Map Collection, Cartography Associates.*

Beaver Wars, seventy years of intertribal warfare, pitted one tribe against the other in a quest for prosperity by trading with the Europeans. Later, these conflicts and alliances became a matter of survival in the face of European dominance, and the natives were forced to choose sides in the white man's wars between the French and English.

This soil has been caught in a tug-of-war since before the forts and cities were built. The Eriez, or cat people, one of the only native groups in North America believed to use poison-tipped arrows, were annihilated or assimilated by the Senecas in 1656. Most Senecas today can trace their lineage to the Eriez. And the history of the Iroquois people is storied with brutal torture, cannibalism and sorcery.

The Iroquois

Expansion by the colonies slowly pushed the natives of New York State to Western New York and beyond. Early native residents were killed, assimilated or driven out and replaced by other stronger tribes, until the Iroquois Confederacy was formed.

The history of the early peoples of the Niagara Region is complex and tied to the formation of the region by blood and warfare. As with many other places in the New World, the Indians here attempted to live and trade with the French and other white settlers. They formed a somewhat symbiotic relationship of give and take. However, greed on the part of the Europeans and a lack of understanding of the tenuous balance between the natives and their environment, coupled with disease for which the natives had no natural immunity, eroded that relationship. The Europeans believed the Indians to be foolish children who needed direction and guidance and could be easily cheated. The natives, having survived years without these invaders, rightfully felt insulted by that position. Not stupid at all, the Indians held conferences and decided for themselves how best to use these Europeans for their own benefit. In truth, there were also greedy natives who sold their land without knowing the consequences for their people or their future.

Simple trade agreements eventually led to the French and British courting the Indians to assist in their conflict, and the Iroquois saw advantage in interacting with the Europeans. The toll that the natives paid for this relationship was great. Disease killed many of the Indians, and later, the introduction of firearms threatened not only them but also the beaver population, by which the natives and Europeans made their livelihood. In addition, their hunting lands disappeared little by little as settlers overstepped the boundaries and took more than what they had purchased.

It was not only by European hands that Indians died. Natives spilled native blood for hunting rights and territory as well. This depleted the tribes of the Iroquois. Intelligent and with a sophisticated system of governance, these depleted tribes did not always slay their enemies but often adopted their fallen foe to replenish their population. Raiding for adoption to acquire personal property or for revenge was commonplace.

It is useless to question why people, native or not, act brutally. The European settlers were appalled and afraid of things outside their own experiences, though it is safe to say that Europeans were not necessarily strangers to torture. The Inquisition, when thousands were tortured and killed in the name of religion, is a good testimony to that. But it has been historically recorded that the Iroquois tortured not only European captives but native captives as well. The Iroquois were known to practice ritualistic cannibalism, and some of their greatest leaders were accused of sorcery. Whether they were, in fact, wicked can be debated, but the Iroquois story of creation is fraught with dark deeds and is said to teach about the balance of good and evil.

Woman Who Fell from the Sky

There are as many variations of this tale as there are storytellers who tell it. This version is a compilation of several of these variations. Some say Sky Woman's husband was angry that she had conceived illegitimately, while others say the Creator deliberately sent a woman to create earth. Either way, the experience was born of violence.

The Sky People lived in harmony far above and beyond the clouds. One day, the Great Tree was pulled up by the roots, leaving a gaping hole in its place. Sky Woman fell through this hole.

Down, down, down she plummeted, with her belly full of new life. She tumbled headfirst at times, arms and legs flailing, desperately trying to grasp at anything to save herself and her unborn child. It was the birds that finally came to ease her fall, and it was upon the back of a great turtle that she landed safely.

Taking seeds she kept in her medicine bag, Sky Woman sprinkled Turtle's back, which had much mud stuck to it, and there grew all the plants she needed to sustain life. It was here that Sky Woman bore a daughter, and this daughter's belly later grew with the child of West Wind. This young woman would soon bear twins, but even while they were in her womb, these twins argued and fought with each other.

The twins pulled each other this way and that, causing such discomfort that their mother often doubled over with the pain of their kicking. Soon, the twins began to argue over how they would be born, one wanting to go one way and the second another. Left-side Twin forced his brother to be born first, but he had decided he would not be born in the usual way. Instead, after his brother was born, Left-side Twin forced his way through his mother's left side and killed her in the process.

The newborns buried their mother, and she became Corn Woman, a major source of food for early natives, providing corn, beans and squash—the Iroquois' "Three Sisters." From her heart grew the sacred tobacco.

The brothers never stopped competing with each other. Right-side Twin created all that is beautiful and peaceful, such as the mountains, streams and plant eaters. Left-side Twin made that which is in opposition: jagged rocks, torrents and predators. Right-side Twin was honest and truthful, whereas Left-side Twin lied and cheated. Right-side created humans, and Left-side ruled over sorcery and healing.

The two brought a delicate balance to the world. There was light and dark, aggression and peace, cooperation and competition. Yet even after they had created the animals and things of this world, the two went on competing until one day, while playing a rather physical game, Right-side Twin killed his brother and threw him over the edge of the world.

Grandmother Sky Woman was angry, and Right-side Twin could not bear her scolding. He cut off his grandmother's head and threw it into the sky, where it became the moon. He threw her body into the sea, where it became the fish. The Iroquois understood the need for both twins in this world and the balance they brought. They celebrated with festivals and dances that honored both the light and the dark. This made up their cycle of life and became a part of their law. It may be that this heritage set in motion the balance of these things in the Niagara Region.

Torture, Cannibalism and Sorcery

The Iroquois methods of torture were varied and gruesome, especially to an outsider. Their justice was not unlike the settlers' frontier justice, which was swift, strong and direct. It certainly sent a loud and clear message. Insubordination and insults were not taken lightly. Captives might be burned alive, disemboweled and sometimes forced to watch as their internal organs were removed, their fingernails pulled out and their eyeballs gauged and left to dangle. To increase the strength of the victors, the living heart was passed and eaten until completely devoured. The remaining body might be hacked into pieces, cooked and eaten for the same reason. This is not unlike ancient cultures that practiced cannibalism and head hunting worldwide, yet it seems particularly disturbing when we realize it was not in ancient times but in fifteenth- and sixteenth-century America.

The Indians took scalps; they were tokens to prove the defeat of an enemy. But the activity touched the colonists in a way that made it difficult for them to stomach. During the French and Indian War and the War for Independence, European military leaders put a price on scalps to encourage their native allies to destroy the enemy. The highest price was for male scalps. To ensure that the Indians killed as few women and children as possible, the British set a lower price for those scalps—but they did have a price, so women and children not directly involved in battle were brutally murdered. The scalps were then traded for money, goods or mere trinkets. Who should we blame for this evil, the natives who were simply doing what

"Iroquois: An Indian War Dance." *Courtesy of U.S. History Images.*

they always did in battle or the Europeans who enacted the bounty to ensure the military victory they wanted?

Regardless of these acts, which seem alien to modern sensitivity, the tribes of the Iroquois Confederacy established a sophisticated legal system that some believe formed a model for what eventually became the law of our great nation. The Great Peacemaker, Dekanawidah, and his contemporary Hiawatha first conceived this law.

Tales are told that Dekanawidah was also a sorcerer who brought about the death of the sun, a solar eclipse to persuade reluctant natives to buy into his idea of unification. The exact dates corresponding to his ideology are confused, and there was at one time during his life a solar eclipse. Whether it timed with his drive for unification or not, the Iroquois Confederacy was formed and became legendary under his leadership.

The law touched on many aspects of Iroquois life, particularly on the forming of its governing body and its intertribal relationships. Iroquois were forbidden to kill other Iroquois by this law, called *Kainerekowa*, the "Great Law of Peace." It allowed them to adopt from outside the nation when needed, which not only increased their population but also eliminated the fear of attack from outsiders.

The Iroquois became allied to the Dutch, who called this law the "Covenant Chain." This military and trade alliance, along with other alliances, became a strong influence throughout the state of New York, in the Niagara Region and beyond.

During the War for Independence, the Iroquois Confederacy was broken, and many of its tribes fled to Canada to resettle there. Most of the Senecas, Onondagas and Tuscaroras remained in the Niagara Region. Once feared by the settlers, the Senecas went on to support them during the War of 1812. Today, these tribes, notably the Senecas, have become an economic force in the region.

RED JACKET

Undeniably one of our history's great orators, Sagoyewatha—or Red Jacket, as the European settlers called him for the red military coat he wore—now rests in Buffalo, New York's Forest Lawn Cemetery along with several other prominent natives. Among these are Young King, Destroy Town, Captain Pollard and his wife and granddaughter, Tall Peter, Little Billy and Ely Parker, a renowned Tonawanda-born American soldier.

Red Jacket's newly restored monument towers above the graves as his words towered above the attempts of the Europeans to dominate his people. Perhaps fittingly, his native name means "He Who Causes Them to be Awake," and today his legacy continues to remind us to be awake or else any one of us, native or not, might lose what freedom we have to someone else. His words, powerful though they may have been, did not keep him from the grave, the Iroquois Confederacy from destruction or the Senecas from losing their lands. And his story is not without a dark shadow.

Red Jacket was once a warrior and was present at the Battle of Oriskany, where General Herkimer and his American militia were ambushed in a ravine on their way to support Fort Stanwix against the British. It is reported that Red Jacket fled this battle. At the massacre of Cherry Valley, Red Jacket is said to have fled also, with the words that it was "too late in the year to fight."

Siding with his people and the British, Red Jacket was most often used as a messenger and did little to contribute to actual combat. For this reason, his fellows branded him a coward in fighting, and even Chief Cornplanter despised this side of his personality. In one instance, Cornplanter even called him a coward in front of his wife. Notorious among the colonists, Joseph Brant labeled Red Jacket a coward when it was discovered that the bloodied axe Red Jacket carried was covered not in the blood of his enemy but in that of a cow. Thus, he was also given the insulting name "Cow Killer."

Perhaps one reason for Red Jacket's reluctance to fight was his belief that the Iroquois Confederacy's decision to side with Britain in the war was a mistake; this would later be proven true, although much the same might have occurred if Britain had been victorious. It's impossible to say. Red Jacket preferred that his people remain neutral. When the British lost, the Iroquois lost as well.

Throughout his life, Red Jacket was passionate about the survival of his nation, and his orations were driven by that passion. It was at the council

Sagoyewatha (Seneca chief Red Jacket). *Courtesy of the Library of Congress Print and Photographs Division.*

fires that he won his renown, reminding white officials that he deserved their respect and missionaries that they should tend to their own before they preached to the Indians. He even told one missionary who attempted to condemn the natives, "First refine the morals of the citizens of Buffalo that they will no longer cheat the Indians."

When the Iroquois Confederacy was disbanded, the Senecas stayed in Western New York. Red Jacket and his followers were among the natives who were allied with the Americans during the War of 1812, the war in which Buffalo was burned. In his older years during this conflict, Red Jacket fought and dispelled his reputation for cowardice, clearing his name and proving himself a good leader. He then spent the rest of his life fighting with words for the rights of the Senecas, urging them not to sell their lands and to protect their heritage. Robert Morris, financier and signer of the Declaration of Independence, contracted with Massachusetts for the purchase of land on March 12, 1791. Red Jacket could not stop the sale of these native lands in the Treaty of Big Tree. The lands purchased by Morris became Western New York.

The Iroquois women held the power in this matter and were supposedly bribed with trinkets by Morris, who then sold much of this acreage to the Holland Land Company, ushering in a new age for New York State, the Indians and the Niagara Region.

Although Red Jacket clashed with Christian missionaries, because his wife was Christian, upon his death on January 20, 1830, he was given burial in the mission cemetery on the old Buffalo Creek reservation. Over the years that followed his death, the missionary cemetery fell into disrepair. It became a grazing ground for wayward cattle. His headstone, a gift from comedian Henry Placide, was chipped away like the relic of a saint, and before long, the grave of Red Jacket and other natives buried there were overgrown and forgotten. They were later crowded by the encroachment of white graves after the land was sold in the Buffalo Creek Treaty.

Following much discussion, in 1885, the remains of Red Jacket and the other Indians, buried beneath years of white settlers' graves, were carefully exhumed and moved honorably to Forest Lawn Cemetery under the supervision of the Buffalo and Erie County Historical Society. While not mentioned in the society's precise description of this event, stories exist that say Red Jacket's body had been removed many years earlier by Indians wishing to follow his last words, which said not to give his body to white men to bury.

Stories claim that his remains, in a plain casket, were taken from one Indian's house to another over the years. These stories are preserved in an article in the *New York Times*, dating July 1, 1884, which posts letters from Ely Parker and William Bryant on the subject. These letters basically express Parker's concerns that the remains should be verified as Red Jacket's and Bryant's response that they were certain of it, one reason being that Ruth Stevenson, daughter of a renowned warrior and chief, claimed to have kept the remains in her possession for several years. She had buried them in an undisclosed place, and as she aged, fearing she might die and the remains would be lost forever, Ruth confided in Reverend Wright, who later saw that they were delivered to the Buffalo and Erie County Historical Society and vaulted safely in a local bank until interment.

Bryant's reply to Parker does mention that perhaps a businessman named Wheeler Hotchkiss, assisted by an undertaker, exhumed Red Jacket, placed his remains in a new coffin and may even have attempted to make a plaster of Paris copy of the skeleton. Rumors were that bits of plaster of Paris still clung to the bones, but the operation was interrupted when an Indian named Daniel Two Guns and several others arrived at Hotchkiss's residence and demanded he release the remains at once. One can only imagine why Hotchkiss would steal Red Jacket's remains, but it was an era of spectacle in which circuses touted such things and people paid to see them. Even artists took advantage of people's curiosity.

Native Witchcraft

Red Jacket is said to have been born somewhere in the Finger Lakes area of New York State, but he spent much of his later years at Buffalo Creek in the Niagara Region. Awarded a peace medal by George Washington and known to be a great speaker, Red Jacket was also accused of sorcery in 1801.

Though magic was not considered evil among the Indians in the same way it was among the Europeans, the use of bad medicine to harm others was not tolerated. Tied to the use of language, sorcery and magic were believed to influence the natural way of things, and since Red Jacket was a very powerful leader by way of his words, this may explain why he was accused. Furthermore, as a powerful leader, he made powerful enemies.

His enemies may have used these accusations as a means of ridding themselves of him.

Other natives also had encounters with witchcraft. Seneca prophet Handsome Lake and a Seneca chief named Tommy Jemmy were touched by sorcery but in different ways. In Tommy Jemmy's case, he was not accused of witchcraft but of murdering a witch, and Red Jacket spoke in his defense during his trial in 1821.

Tommy Jemmy was on trial for slitting the throat of a Seneca woman. There was no dispute over whether or not he did it. He didn't deny it. In fact, he claimed he was carrying out the Indian law that said a person who was a witch must be killed, and the woman had been declared a witch. This woman had supposedly tended an ill man, who died under strange circumstances. Tommy Jemmy killed her on a reservation near Buffalo. His trial with the State of New York was not about whether he committed the deed but whether New York State had any jurisdiction to bring Jemmy to trial when he was a member of a sovereign Indian nation.

Red Jacket, always outspoken with his passion to secure his people's continued freedom, spoke on Jemmy's behalf. If he did not, in his mind, he would have been agreeing that the white man's law held sway over the Indian's, and thus he would be helping the state take away more of their rights.

Testifying was no easy matter for Red Jacket. The court called into question his belief in God, or lack thereof, and his standing among his people—whether he was even qualified to testify. Red Jacket overcame these doubts and threw back at the prosecutor the fact that it hadn't been all that long ago that the settlers had done the very same thing as Tommy Jemmy during the Salem witch hunts. Nearly speechless and certainly unable to disregard Red Jacket's defense, the case was referred to the Supreme Court. In the end, the case against Tommy Jemmy was dismissed.

This was not the first time Red Jacket spoke on behalf of a Seneca brought before the New York State court. Prior to the trial of Tommy Jemmy, a Seneca man was accused of killing a New York State citizen. The attorney who prosecuted this case was district attorney John Spencer. Red Jacket also managed to get this man acquitted, and after the trial, he approached John Spencer, confronting him with the fact that the slain man had been Spencer's own brother. When Spencer denied this, Red Jacket accused him of taking a bribe to prosecute. John Spencer acquiesced, and the Great Orator Red Jacket won the victory. Even John Spencer is said to have admired the Seneca leader after that. In fact, John Spencer was so affected by his experience with Red Jacket during that trial that he acted as advisor to Red Jacket in the Tommy Jemmy trial. And it was John Spencer who convinced the court that since the murder took place on Seneca lands, the court had no jurisdiction over it.

The Trial of Red Jacket

Can you economize on something like a Native American being tried for sorcery? Artist John Mix Stanley did, but then, he wasn't alone. Stanley put his painting, *The Trial of Red Jacket*, on the circuit just as many other artists of his time, charging people to come and view it. In entrepreneurial terms, this was an ingenious way for the artist to make money from his labors and create for himself a legacy, since we can still view this painting today. It is now in the possession of the Buffalo Erie County Historical Society, not a shabby bargain on the society's part either. The painting is very beautiful and has amazing details, even though the artist took some liberties. The manner of dress of the Indians present in this painting is not solely representative of the Niagara Region or the Senecas. Whether the event unfolded as he painted it or if so many were present at the trial is not documented, but the trial itself is believed to have taken place.

Stanley used this work to show his knowledge on a variety of tribes throughout the United States, and as was common during his era, this painting also became a tool for educating the masses about the country's heritage. The painting predates the common use of photography and cinema and also served as a form of entertainment. Created by the artist between 1862 and 1868, it was draped in velvet and displayed with footlights. The public paid pennies to view it and wonder about the story it portrayed.

It isn't known whether Red Jacket was a sorcerer, but a fellow Seneca chief and prophet, Handsome Lake, accused Red Jacket, who was also outspoken about the white man's religion. The orator's passion placed him between these two factions. Red Jacket was opposed to both the Christian missionaries' attempts to win over the Indians and to Handsome Lake, whose religious teachings led Red Jacket to call him an imposter.

Red Jacket, Seneca war chief. *Courtesy of the Library of Congress Print and Photographs Division.*

Handsome Lake used this opportunity to accuse Red Jacket of witchcraft. He also pointed a finger at Red Jacket's inability to stave off the sale of Indian lands to the whites and even blamed him for being directly involved in those sales. Of course, Red Jacket's long-standing rivalry with another powerful leader named Cornplanter didn't help. It was Cornplanter who spurred Handsome Lake into the accusation. The punishment under native law for these crimes was death. Red Jacket had to speak for himself on this occasion. He held his audience spellbound for three hours. The Indians present who had the right to determine Red Jacket's fate were divided in their opinions. Finally, Red Jacket won, and Cornplanter was diminished.

Code of Handsome Lake

Cornplanter, half brother to Handsome Lake (both uncles to Red Jacket), fell out of favor over time. Handsome Lake's fervor was not entirely bad for the Indians. He was against the alcoholism that threatened the moral fiber of his people. Many had taken to drinking to mask the grief of losing so much, and he himself had nearly succumbed to alcohol before he had his prophetic visions in 1799. In these visions, four messengers came and showed him the downfall of his nation. Primary among these were alcoholism and witchcraft. He claimed fire would destroy the world if the people did not follow this code of conduct. Handsome Lake thought of himself as a messenger of the Great Spirit, and a cult formed around him. Eventually, his overzealous pursuit of witches and the murder of several lost him support among the general Indian population. Still, he maintained followers and regained his favor during the War of 1812.

One of his teachings was that the spirit of a person is divided upon death, one piece going to the eternal and the other remaining on Earth. These remaining ghosts, who want to be near their loved ones, might torment them and inhabit them in an effort to be close. Therefore, it is not a good idea to speak the name of the dead. Iroquois women performed the Ghost Dance to satisfy them.

The Code of Handsome Lake was entrenched in the Niagara Region and is still recognized as a significant piece of Seneca history today.

Blood and Sinew

Immigration

After the French and Indian War, with the British in control here and their Indian allies living peacefully in the shadow of their forts, colonists from the East began a slow movement westward via Lakes Ontario and Erie and overland along the Mohawk River. Travel was slow and dangerous, with points west of Albany still being considered wilderness. The Mohawk Valley became peppered with small settlements until the War for Independence, but settlement had stopped short of reaching the Niagara frontier. During the war, fighting, raiding and conflict among neighbors raged throughout New England and along the Mohawk, but the Niagara Region was firmly held by the British so that turmoil was at a minimum. The conflict was distant.

Yet Fort Niagara was a staging ground for the British. The waterways made it convenient for supplies and men to be shipped in all directions. Such a stronghold in America allowed the British to control these waterways. Under the gates of Fort Niagara passed some of the most notorious enemies to the Americans during the War for Independence. Among them were John Butler and his Rangers, who harassed settlements, killing, burning and taking scalps; John Johnson, William Johnson's son and an Indian agent; and Red Jacket and Cornplanter in their warrior years. William Johnson, who had taken the fort during the French and Indian War, and future Mohawk chief Joseph Brant, then very young, were also within the walls of the fort at one time. Joseph Brant's sister later married William Johnson.

But for all the times the fort passed back and forth from French to British to American control, it was not the English or the French—or, in the end, the Indians—who influenced this region the most. Yes, many streets, cities, and parks have French or Indian names, and they are part of our rich heritage. But it was the Italians, Germans, Poles and Irish, after the scars of war healed, who left the deepest, most lasting marks. They came overland, by way of the Erie Canal and on the railways that once crisscrossed this region. They came from their homelands in Europe through New York City, following the work that was created by industry, which in later years was drawn from the hydroelectric power of the mighty Niagara River. During the American Civil War, slaves settled here, and in modern times, people have fled war-torn countries to come here from Israel, Africa, South America and the Middle East. The arms of the Niagara have gathered many people, mostly in peace and harmony—but not always.

North Side, South Side, East Side, West Side

Every city seems to have them, those districts separated by customs and cultures. People cannot help but be drawn together by shared ideals and experiences, by family and by work. Buffalo, New York, has such districts as well.

Settlement began with explorers and missionaries in the 1600s, and by the late 1700s, the earliest settlers were building as close to waterways as was safely possible. Buffalo Village grew up on what was called "the Terrace," twenty some feet above Lake Erie. Pockets of settlements then expanded around the civilized places, around shops and businesses and along well-traveled roads to support the needs of travelers. Burned to the ground by the British in the War of 1812, Buffalo drew hardy settlers who returned after the British were defeated to rebuild what they had started.

Eventually, in the mid-1800s, following the creation of "Clinton's Ditch" (the Erie Canal), these neighborhoods became grouped by culture and economics. There were the haves and the have-nots, the business owners and the workers. This last group often lived in substandard company housing or tenements, and the wealthy moved inland away from the stench of industry. Buffalo had class and it had ruffians. The city was well storied and diverse.

The districts have changed and shifted over the years, but at one time, the Italians were prevalent on the west side, the Irish on the south side, the Germans and Poles on the east side and a large Jewish population on the north side. Today, these areas are Hispanic and African American, with a mixture of other cultures thrown in. Very few of the original cultural centers remain, but there are still pockets of the old neighborhoods with strong ethnic ties. Buffalo's north side is now home to a small but strong Italian community. The Irish of South Buffalo have their own cultural center and Saint Patrick's Day parade.

The Irish Are Coming! The Irish Are Coming!

Driven from their homeland by the Great Hunger, often called the Irish Potato Famine, between 1845 and 1852, over one million Irish emigrated, changing Irish history. While the blight of crops was environmental, one-third of the Irish population relied on potatoes for sustenance. This trouble was attributed to less than adequate British governance, which could not stave off the lack of jobs or food or overcome the pride of a people who not only did not willingly accept British rule but also did not like the English church. Laws took away the rights of the Irish people, especially those who were Catholic. Catholic Irish could not own land or be educated, vote, lease land, hold political office or, under some circumstances, enter a profession. Historically, this condition is one that sparked later nationalist movements in the country.

America offered employment opportunities and the freedoms so desired by Irish families. Many sought comfort in America, and the Niagara Region was a natural extension of what was available to these new arrivals. Though many settled in the shadow of Lady Liberty and stayed in New York City, thousands came to Buffalo, New York.

Of the immigrants settling here, the Irish were among the first in Buffalo. A small Irish neighborhood sprang up on the Flats at Buffalo's waterfront and was well settled by 1817. Following the Great Hunger, those who came here found a booming grain port city. Over time, the Irish would become

Immigrant boat. *Courtesy of the Library of Congress Print and Photographs Division.*

key laborers as Buffalo grew into a major shipping, railway and industrial center. Population estimates neared over ten thousand Irish residents by the late 1800s. They settled in what was known as Buffalo's First Ward, in the canal district near the places they worked. In fact, the men who worked in the grain elevators were mostly Irish. The Irish of the First Ward lived in poor shacks under the worst hygienic conditions. When the cholera outbreak of the mid-1800s visited Buffalo, hundreds died—mostly poor laborers, and many were Irish. Irishmen also played a prominent role in digging the Erie Canal and, through that, helped give birth to the American West.

Canal Street

The western terminus of the Erie Canal at Buffalo might be considered the birthplace for many other great cities to the west. People arriving via the canal were often traveling to settle in the West. Some did stay, and some worked here on Canal Street, later known by many other nicknames like

There were many forms of entertainment on Canal Street. Men with full pockets often left with nothing, if they left at all. *Courtesy of the author.*

Little Italy, Dante Place, Five Points and the Hooks. It was located above what was commonly known during the 1800s as the Flats, a strip of low, boggy land below the city terrace.

From the completion of the canal in 1825, the Canal District was a thriving and dangerous place. As wicked as any pirate-infested Caribbean island, the Canal District was peopled with rough sailors, thieves and prostitutes. People of respectable nature stayed away. Canal nightlife was for gambling, smuggling and burlesque. Let the respectable people have their fancy theater and finery; the denizens of Canal Street lived on the edge. As long as these activities stayed below the terrace, polite society looked the other way.

Canal Street was originally the site of Buffalo Village, very near Buffalo Creek, the former Seneca village, and ran parallel to the Erie Canal. Commerce grew along the canal, with supplies coming in from the East. People, disease, vermin and crime traveled the canal. Some called the Canal District infected, while others called it infested. By 1893, there were no fewer than seven houses of ill repute and five saloons located there. If you wanted it, it had a price on Canal Street and could be bought. Woe to the man gaming in the Hooks with heavy pockets on payday. There were plenty of ways to spend your hard-earned cash on alcohol, entertainment and carnal pleasures and an equal number of ways to have it involuntarily disappear. It was not unusual to wake with a headache and empty pockets in the Canal District, if one was fortunate enough to wake at all.

Considering it was the mid- to late 1800s, the risqué activities in the playhouses and saloons make one wonder how advanced today's society really is. Famous for her work on major theater circuits but said to have fallen on hard times, a sailor once said he saw Kitty O'Neill dance naked on a pedestal. Before one disqualifies that as so much rumor of the day, it is best to note that there are many documented stories of the ladies of the night dancing bare bottomed and flashing thighs to tuck some money into their garters. Also, men were pressed into service after losing their hard-earned cash in games of poker or perhaps to a pickpocket. One Captain Cole even went so far as to relate that a particular alehouse had a back room where men were waylaid and thrown unconscious to drown in the river, claiming to have escaped this adventure himself.

Built to a great extent by Irishmen, the canal helped increase Buffalo's diversity. The west side of Buffalo, a portion of which is known as Black Rock for the natural color of the rock on which it is built, became home to many Irish immigrants who wished to live near their places of employment after moving out of the Flats. However, the turn of the century brought a change for the Canal District, ushering in the age of industry and immigration to service that industry by way of the railroads. By the early twentieth century, the Canal District had grown into a predominantly Italian neighborhood when many Italians were forced from their homeland by famine and high taxes. Many of these new families came from Sicily.

The Irish neighborhoods gradually moved into South Buffalo, and their original neighborhood on the canal became peopled with Italians. This is when Canal Street came to be known as Dante Place or Little Italy. The district slowly morphed into a more family-oriented neighborhood. Although poor, with many people living in tenement houses, the focus of these Italian immigrants was on hard work and not on debauchery. Irish families had long since migrated south of the city, out of this district, for similar reasons.

Irish Mythology in America

Once, in Ancient Ireland, there roamed a mythical band of mighty warriors known as the Fianna, or the Fenians. Each man of the Fianna was chosen for strength and courage and was trained as a champion. Founded by Conn of the Hundred Battles, high king of Ireland or Ari, the Fianna were tested and true and lived apart from the rest of society. Answering to the Ari, many gained legendary fame. They were the elite and were charged with keeping the high king's peace.

To become a Fenian warrior, the chosen passed a series of tests not unlike the jumping-in ceremonies for potential members in today's street gangs. They had to run through the forest without breaking any branches or leaving a footprint. They had to stand in a waist-deep hole and fight off other Fianna with a blackthorn stick, jump over branches as tall as a man and memorize poetry. Becoming a Fianna was a challenge and an honor. The tales of the Fenian warriors are among the most treasured stories in Ireland. Ancient Ireland is peopled with great warriors and mystical beings, and these stories and ideals followed the Irish wherever their paths led them, including to the Americas.

IRISH GANGS ON THE STREETS OF BUFFALO

The movie *Gangs of New York* portrays the area of New York City known as the Five Points during the mid-nineteenth century. Very much on the edge, stretched and stressed to the maximum following the Irish Potato Famine, this region was a powder keg waiting for someone to light the fuse. The poorest of the poor lived there in squalid conditions in the tenement houses. The Irish ruled New York City's Five Points for nearly twenty years. With no indoor plumbing, livestock in the streets and people crammed into one-room flats, life was uncomfortable to say the least.

Exterior of 260 Terrace Street, Buffalo, New York. Several Italian families, who spent the summer in the Cannery District, lived here. *Courtesy of the Library of Congress Print and Photographs Division.*

These new urban gangs were more like social or political clubs, with Irish of common beliefs and interests banding together. Often hotheaded, they would pick fights with one another, most often fistfights. This was also true of Buffalo's Irish, who, after all, came from the same country and often had lived for a time in New York City.

Buffalo's Five Points, the Flats, was a mirror image of New York's Irish neighborhood on a smaller scale. Hardworking but poor, the residents tried to make the best of what they had, but it was not uncommon for daily life to spill into the streets. Still surrounded by houses of ill repute, Irish families lived, worked and went to church in their neighborhood. They had pride in their heritage. Because they had come here to find work, they guarded their jobs with fierce determination. This eventually exploded and led to an assault on the "Negro Block," not so much because of bigotry but because of employment concerns.

Known formally as the Union Block, this area along the canal's waterfront held several African American–owned businesses, including the infamous Dug's Dive, a tavern run by former slave William Douglas. These establishments flourished by catering to sailors and laborers of a rough nature. At Dug's Dive, patrons sometimes included escaped or emancipated slaves on their way to freedom in Canada. The Union Block was really much like a series of row houses, three stories high. There were African American residences, businesses, brothels and rooms for let. Many believe this block was a stop on the Underground Railroad as well. This makes perfect sense, as this block was right on the waterfront, with the river, canal and lake easily accessible and within visual distance of the Canadian border.

The year was 1863. Civil war tore the nation, pitting Northern states against Southern states, brother against brother, abolitionist against slave owner. While the war hadn't begun as a war against slavery, President Abraham Lincoln saw the issue of slavery as an excellent way to spark more interest in a floundering military force. It did help, and many new soldiers joined the cause, but it wasn't enough to win the war. Lincoln's army desperately needed more men, and the best way to get them was to institute a draft. This did not sit well with many citizens—not because they didn't love their country, but because they didn't want to be forced into service, and many needed to remain in current jobs to support families. Adding to this frustration was the emancipation of slaves and the flood of freed slaves moving north. New York State governor Horacio Seymour openly stated that the liberation of so many slaves would force the country into military despotism. It was conscription and an outrage!

During the spring of 1863, military enrollers went door to door throughout the city of Buffalo searching for men of appropriate age, those twenty to forty-five. Families with enough money could simply buy their way out of the draft, or a man of means might choose someone to go in his place. If you were poor, you had no choice but to go. This is when the Civil War became a war of class as far as the average man was concerned. Later that summer, Governor Seymour further outraged his constituents by telling them that the country was dangerously close to collapse, with human rights being violated left and right. Former U.S. president Franklin Pierce gave a similar speech. The newspapers did not hide this information; in fact, they carried it widely. The rumor mills were working overtime, and poor, hardworking men—especially the Irish—took up the slogan, "A rich man's war but a poor man's fight." For the Irishmen, having come from a country of British overseers, this lit the fuse. In fact, many Irish were fighting in the war, and this felt like a further slap in the face.

Two years into the Civil War, President Lincoln signed the Emancipation Proclamation, which went into effect in January 1863. Rumors spread that the president had ordered a draft of men to shore up his army. The first Battle of Bull Run had taken many lives, and the government tried to get volunteers to enlist. When that didn't work, it decided to use the draft to spur more into signing voluntarily. The first names drawn were the names of men who were laborers, and that furthered deepened growing anger. Additionally, the United States government refused to let blacks join the military; at the same time, Negroes were moving northward in droves, with Buffalo becoming a staging ground for travel over the border to Canada.

In Buffalo in 1863, the issue exploded. Fighting broke out on the docks of Buffalo's harbor. Reports of how it began are sketchy at best. Apparently, there were two separate occasions when trouble erupted, once in July just two weeks before the infamous draft riots of New York City and once in August. While little is known of what happened behind closed doors leading up to the actual event, one can speculate, and the story might have gone something like the following, with groups of laborers, mostly Irish, huddled in secret.

"Why couldn't they just let us be?" said one man, slamming his fist on the table hard enough to throw its contents across the room.

"Let us go about our work as we always have!" shouted another. "After all, we came to this country to escape this kind of tyranny!"

A third voice chimed in, "Aye, he's right. I'm a hardworkin' man and never shirked my duty, but if I'm not here, who will look after my family?"

A murmur circled the room as man after man agreed. The draft was unfair, and they would strike. A plan was hatched.

The white laborers on Buffalo's waterfront went on strike in July 1863 in protest of low wages, but the draft was an underlying cause. With so many eager and strong black men moving north, it was not difficult for the bosses to replace the strikers. The docks of Buffalo fueled a nation, and the bosses would not let a few upstarts bring the whole system to a screeching halt. They simply offered work to those who were willing, and the blacks were willing. The scabs angered white laborers. The Irishmen were willing to fight in the Civil War to help these men of color but not at the cost of losing their jobs to the very men they were trying to set free. Summer heat, hotheaded Irish tempers and the need to survive make for a powerful mixture.

On July 6, two days after Governor Seymour's inflammatory speech, an angry mob of Irish workers indiscriminately attacked any and all blacks they found, killing at least two. One can only imagine that they came armed with fists, boards and crowbars. They were an angry mob bent on taking matters into their own hands. The Union Block, or "Negro Block," was their goal. Rioters pushed their way past police and bystanders as they marched like a wall of fire toward the district and surrounded the block.

We can never know the intentions of these rioters when they arrived at the Union Block. They certainly attacked blacks along the way, and perhaps they intended to pull men, women and children from their apartments and businesses and burn the buildings. After all, that was what happened in New York City just days later. Had the police not been able to stop Buffalo rioters, Buffalo's fate might have been the same. Yet troubles were not over.

It was an early August day when Irish dockworkers once more spilled into the streets of Buffalo's waterfront. Most likely, they headed first to the bosses to demand enforcement of the strike. Any black scab in their way was a target. Or perhaps they intended to march on the draft offices and the homes of city officials, as their brothers in New York had done. Whatever

The scabs appeal to Justice. *Courtesy of the Library of Congress Print and Photographs Division.*

their goal, it was an open anthill and a menace to the city. Perhaps they would even march on city hall.

City officials immediately issued police and a volunteer company to help quench the inflamed rabble as they crossed Main Street's business district into a predominately black neighborhood. It took several hours for officials, and a militia regiment just returned from the riots in New York to contain the violence.

The Fenian Brotherhood

The Civil War was undeniably one of the country's most perilous times. Historians believe it defined who we are as a nation. Except for a few raids, actual wartime fighting never made it farther north than Gettysburg. Yet Buffalo played a role in the war, with supplies and men pouring in and out by its railways and waterways. New York State, including Buffalo, also supplied many of its finest as soldiers, too. Many died, some returned. As is the case in history, if one looks at wars throughout the world, there were those veterans who only knew how to soldier. They found peacetime difficult. Approximately one million men were suddenly unemployed.

The end of the Civil War left many men without work and purpose. While most went home to family, some continued to band together, even at a distance. Many of these men were Irish who had fought during the war in mixed companies but also in Irish regiments. The war ended in 1865, but for these Irishmen, the cause of freedom was still an issue in their homeland. In fact, Irish nationalism was at a high point.

Irish immigrants left Ireland following a dream. It was a dream of a better life, with food and shelter and the right to choose how they would live. No wonder so many became abolitionists, fighting with the North in the American Civil War. Their own country had been under English subjugation in varying degrees since the twelfth century. Their ancestors had lived through the 1600s, when the English set up Protestant colonies on Irish Catholic soil, and the late 1600s, when they rebelled, attempting to form an independent Irish state. These Irish Americans themselves had fled famine brought on by poor governance under British rule. No wonder they had no qualms about a new rebellion—or at least a continued one on a new front. The Irish Americans would invade Canada.

The Fenian Brotherhood originates in 1798 with the United Irishmen, a political organization that rebelled against British rule and was suppressed into a secret revolutionary society. The Fenian name came into use in 1858 after many of its leaders and followers fled Ireland to Paris, where they found sympathy for their cause. America was another destination. Two important leaders of the Fenian Brotherhood were among those fugitives. James Stephens stayed in Paris, while John O'Mahony continued on to America.

The brotherhood was already an underground movement in Ireland and Paris prior to the first shots of the American Civil War. Irish Americans were divided in their support, with many wanting to be loyal to both the United States and the Fenian cause. By the time O'Mahony came to the United States, the war here had begun, and longtime plans for raising an army of Irish American rebels had to be placed on hold, as these men were otherwise detained in their own battles.

Even though plans had to be placed on hold, O'Mahony managed to stir up interest, as did agents who moved freely among soldiers in their camps. Once the war ended, the Fenians went into action.

The plan was not roughshod; it was well formed by veterans, including officers of the Civil War. Knowing what was happening in their homeland

and wanting to give aid—and perhaps feeling that they had supplies and manpower at the ready—the Fenian Brotherhood stood poised to strike. Their leaders had been waiting for the moment when these soldiers would be sent home from service. Their brethren in England and Ireland had failed, but they felt that some event would occur in their plans that would bring the United States government itself to their side—and indeed, no one in the United States government seemed to do anything to stop their plans. Little known to them, the British did have spies and secret service agents among their fold, and this was key to the outcome of their efforts.

Stephens and O'Mahony had many disagreements about how the organizations in Ireland and America should be structured, and American geography, being more spread out at that time than that of Ireland, made it difficult for O'Mahony to command such an organization. To further complicate their efforts, they did not gain support from the Catholic Church. This made it hard but not impossible to gain members. Thousands of young Irish men joined their ranks. The Fenians raised membership and money with the sale of five-dollar Fenian bonds. Irish Americans with hearts as big as the ocean that separated them from their homeland opened their purses and raided their secret stashes. With these funds, the Fenians purchased arms and other supplies for their army. They even went so far as to elect William Robert, an opponent of O'Mahony, as their president. He in turn appointed General T.W. Sweeny as his secretary of war. The new Irish Republic was founded—a country within a country—surprisingly on the tail of the Civil War. An interesting note is that this organization is the only one in history that openly armed, drilled and attempted to seize Canada as a separate nation within the nation.

These veteran soldiers created a very elaborate chain of command. The Fenian Brotherhood was composed of circles with any number of men as members, and the circles had officers who answered to a centre. That centre took commands from a state centre, who was appointed by O'Mahony. Furthermore, each member paid a small fee to join and took an oath of allegiance:

> *I, …, in the presence of Almighty God, do solemnly swear allegiance to the Irish Republic, now virtually established; and that I will do my very utmost, at every risk, while life lasts, to defend its independence and integrity; and, finally, that I will yield implicit obedience in all things, not contrary to the*

> *laws of God* [or "the laws of morality"], *to the commands of my superior officers. So help me God. Amen.*

The Fenian capitol was located in New York City, establishing the organization as a national power, but the second largest city in the state had a circle of the Fenian Brotherhood awaiting its marching orders too. That city was Buffalo, New York.

All the King's Horses

On June 1–3, 1866, the Fenians set up staging points all along the Canadian border with a central point in Buffalo. Intent on conquering Canada, the Irish, under their president, William Robert, planned to seize it and hold it hostage until Britain removed itself from Ireland. The Fenians plotted a series of raids that would take control of transportation and cut off communications in Canada itself. One point from which they would strike was Buffalo, New York, with its strategic waterways, railroads and proximity to British forts across the border. John O' Neill, who was to take several hundred Fenians from Buffalo to Canada and secure the position there while waiting for expected Fenian reinforcements to arrive, commanded this position. These reinforcements are said to have been fifty thousand men and a fleet of ships. Instead, he met enemy reinforcements of British regulars and Canadian militia.

In his lengthy account of historical events, *Troublous Times in Canada: A History of the Fenian Raids of 1866 and 1870*, John A. MacDonald states that this was a most dangerous time for Canada. The nation was young, vulnerable and spread out, and its population was sparse. Canada was not yet officially declared independent (this would happen in 1867).

It was no secret that Irish forces with American ties were planning and massing. Yet the Canadian shores off Buffalo were vacant of Canadian soldiers. The nearest major British force was miles away at Port Colborne, with a smaller force at Chippawa. Old Fort Erie was long abandoned, and the village of Fort Erie was vulnerable and a target of that first invasion. The United States government continued to turn a blind eye to the movement, except to send the USS *Michigan* to patrol the waters. This was the first iron-hulled ship in the U.S. Navy.

Other problems plagued Fenian plans, including disagreements in the leadership between O'Mahony and Robert. A preempted and unsuccessful strike by O'Mahony against Campo Bello Island at the mouth of Sainte Croix River in New Brunswick almost crushed the movement before it began, but President Robert and his secretary of war, T.W. Sweeny, did not delay in taking action. In May 1866, they began a series of diversions intended to draw attention away from the crucial St. Lawrence. Attacks were plotted at many spots along the Canadian border, including the one that came from Buffalo.

A train pulled into the outskirts of Buffalo slow enough for Colonel O'Neill's men to leap off before it came to the station. They meant to avoid all contact with the local police and any busybody who might ask questions or report them. Even more troubling, O'Neill had received word that the USS *Michigan* was moored in Buffalo's harbor and would soon begin blockading the waterways.

Fenian circles from Buffalo met O'Neill's troops and smuggled them into the city, hiding them in the warehouses, barns and cellars of South Buffalo. Smuggled in on furniture wagons and other means, arms and supplies were unloaded secretly and stashed for later use. Spies reported Fenian movement throughout New England and along the border to Canada, and citizens noticed an increase in the number of strangers in their communities. They came from Tennessee, Ohio, Indiana and other western states, and most were Irishmen. The Fenians had been prepared for this. General Sweeny had apparently sent several contingents on missions designed to confuse spies and U.S. officials. He had several companies of Fenians who simply pretended to be "up to something," while the real deal assembled and prepared. However, the mayor of Buffalo, Chandler J. Wells, did his civic duty by sending a warning to Toronto and Hamilton and by placing Buffalo police on alert.

By May 31, almost everyone with common sense believed that the Fenians were massing in Buffalo for an attack across the Niagara River. British forces were on alert, and orders to march had been given. The force at Port Colborne housed militia from Toronto and the Niagara Peninsula, among other places, with British regulars on their way. Citizens in Canadian cities and towns along the border were to be vigilant. St. Catherine's was tense due to its border proximity.

In the predawn hours of June 1, O'Neill marched his force of about eight hundred men, including Buffalo's Seventh IRA Regiment, along the Niagara River to Black Rock. Though he was given no maps of Canada to guide him once he arrived, his orders were clear: he was to secure an encampment on Canadian soil and ready things for the larger force that was to follow. When reinforcements arrived and everything was in place, the Fenians would head to Port Colborne and take the Welland Canal.

O'Neill had already begun to form a strategy. When they landed, he would immediately set up a picket line with guards and send a party to cut telegraph wires and shut down the railroad. But first, they had to cross the river and take the village of Fort Erie, which proved rather easy, as luck would have it.

First, O'Neill had to take his troops past Fort Porter in Black Rock (now the site of the Peace Bridge). Soldiers stationed there watched but did not impede his march, even though Major Durr of the fort did take a silent head count of men and supplies and made a report to his superiors. Nonetheless, the soldiers made no move to stop the Fenians, and it appeared the whole of the United States government looked the other way. Some speculate they did so because the British had given aid to the South during the recent Civil War. Whatever the reason, the lack of United States protest to Fenian activities was blatantly obvious.

O'Neill's troops left the Pratt's Furnace dock in Black Rock on barges used for ferrying employees across the river. The troops were not uniformly dressed; some wore green and donned black bowlers, while veterans wore their old uniforms. It was not a rabble-rousing mob that landed without incident on the shore of Canada at Fort Erie. They were well armed, with officers having swords and pistols. Rifled muskets were at the ready.

Fort Erie citizens were sound asleep in the wee hours until one of O'Neill's men, overcome with zeal, leapt from his barge and plunged their flag into the ground with a loud shout of elation. Now they had been announced, but without proper military support, there was little the citizens of the village could do.

O'Neill sent one of his officers, Captain Starr, with the Fenian contingent of Kentuckians and men from Indiana to secure old Fort Erie and handle the telegraphs and railroads along the way. He himself would command the New York, Ohio and Tennessean contingent to secure the village, as previously planned. All were ordered to commandeer any horses they might find. Scouts went about their business too and brought O'Neill a mount and news of a Canadian force on the march to meet him. This included possibly three thousand men—Canadian militia and British regulars, members of the Queen's Own Rifles!

It was still only about four o'clock in the morning, and by five o'clock, Captain Starr was embedded in the fort itself, and one of his Kentucky captains set out to find a railroad bridge to destroy. Village leader Dr. Kempson was ordered to find food for O'Neill's troops, and O'Neill's men were at work creating an earthwork trench at Newbigging Farm on Frenchman's Creek. Newbigging Farm became an outpost, fortified with the earthworks and bullet screens. These screens were sections of sloping fences supported by dirt and sod and had been found most effective when Starr marched in Sherman's campaign to the sea.

The farm, nestled along Frenchman's Creek and the Niagara River, formed a "U" and made a very protected encampment. There could be no mistake: this was a real invasion by a real army.

The Fenian secretary of war issued the following proclamation, reminiscent (somewhat comically) of a cartoon where men from Earth meet those of Mars with the hail, "We come in peace." Canadians were neither persuaded nor amused.

> *To the people of British America:*
> *We come among you as foes of British rule in Ireland. We have taken up the sword to strike down the oppressors' rod, to deliver Ireland from the tyrant, the despoiler, the robber. We have registered our oaths upon the altar of our country in the full view of heaven and sent out our vows to the throne of Him who inspired them. Then, looking about us for an enemy, we find him here, here in your midst, where he is most vulnerable and convenient to our strength…We have no issue with the people of these Provinces, and wish to have none but the most friendly relations. Our weapons are for the oppressors of Ireland. Our bows shall be directed only against the power of England; her privileges alone shall we invade, not yours. We do not propose to divest you of a solitary right you now enjoy…We are here neither as murderers, nor robbers, for plunder and spoliation* [sic]. *We are here as the Irish army of liberation, the friends of liberty against despotism, of democracy*

against aristocracy, of people against their oppressors. In a word, our war is with the armed powers of England, not with the people, not with these Provinces. Against England, upon land and sea, till Ireland is free…To Irishmen throughout these Provinces we appeal in the name of seven centuries of British inequity and Irish misery and suffering, in the names of our murdered sires, our desolate homes, our desecrated alters [sic], *our million of famine graves, our insulted name and race—to stretch forth the hand of brotherhood in the holy cause of fatherland, and smite the tyrant where we can. We conjure you, our countrymen, who from misfortune inflicted by the very tyranny you are serving, or from any other cause, have been forced to enter the ranks of the enemy, not to be willing instruments of your country's death or degradation. No uniform, and surely not the blood-dyed coat of England, can emancipate you from the natural law that binds your allegiance to Ireland, to liberty, to right, to justice. To the friends of Ireland, of freedom, of humanity, of the people, we offer the olive branch of these and the honest grasp of friendship. Take it Irishmen, Frenchmen, American, take it all and trust it…We wish to meet with friends; we are prepared to meet with enemies. We shall endeavor to merit the confidence of the former, and the latter can expect from us but the leniency of a determined though generous foe and the restraints and relations imposed by civilized warfare.*

T.W. Sweeney.
Major General commending the armies of Ireland

Meanwhile, back on American shores, U.S. officials and Buffalo's British consul tried to assess the situation to decide if it was of any significant consequence, while United State's howitzers were loaded onto patrol boats preparing to carry out orders to secure the Niagara waters. The uncertainty of all of this must have caused a great deal of stress in both countries. Although British spies reported what the Fenians had planned, officials must have been surprised at the precision and efficiency with which those plans were carried out. That was, no doubt, unexpected.

It was nearly 3:00 p.m. The *Michigan* steamed along the Niagara River, acting as a base for the patrol boats. Reports came that the Fenians in the village of Fort Erie were forming up, but little else could be told. Even as darkness fell, O'Neill still awaited further orders from his commanders in the

States, and he was already reassured that the opposing forces were in place at Port Colborne, with many more than the original estimate of three thousand having arrived via railway throughout the day. O'Neill's reinforcements weren't coming; the USS *Michigan* saw to that. He was on his own, and he couldn't just sit there waiting for the onslaught.

By 9:00 p.m., Frenchman's Bridge was burning. O'Neill and his army piled it high with useless supplies, some having been set aside for Canadian recruits they couldn't get and reinforcements that never came. At least in this way he could ensure that the enemy would not get the supplies and that nobody else could cross that bridge. Perhaps this would divert attention from his column as they marched toward Port Colborne. The watchman onboard the *Michigan* saw the flames and reported it to his commander, Captain Bryson. The USS *Michigan* readied its guns.

Word of Fenian movement reached the British commander at Chippawa several miles northwest of Frenchman's Creek on the Niagara River. Port Colborne was several miles southwest of O'Neill's position and almost due west of Fort Erie, which lay south of O'Neill's new encampment. O'Neill had little reconnaissance north of his location and planned to march his men north along the river to Black Creek and then head west toward Colborne. The militia in Colborne knew that Black Creek lay approximately midpoint and that O'Neill's army was headed that way (his fires had signaled as much). They contemplated a way to use the British in Chippawa to sandwich the Fenians and defeat them. When O'Neill reached Black Creek in the night, he moved his men toward the high ground of Lime Ridge, near a small town named Ridgeway. Unknown to O'Neill, he was about to make history.

Lieutenant Colonel J. Stoughton Dennis commanded the troops at Port Colborne, and Colonel George John Peacocke had the troops at Chippawa. Peacocke's plan was to trap the Fenians with the full force of the Canadian might, but Dennis wanted to keep some of his men at Port Colborne to defend the canal. Combined, these two contingencies numbered close to three thousand. O'Neill was outnumbered nearly three to one.

Indeed, leaving troops at the port, Colonel Dennis took eighty men by way of steam tug to block any Fenian retreat at Fort Erie. He did this at 3:30 a.m. on June 2, after sending word to Peacocke of his decision. Colonel Peacocke's reply, stating that he disapproved of the plan, never made it to Dennis on time. Dennis was already underway. Lieutenant Colonel Albert

Booker at Port Colborne was instructed to go ahead and proceed as planned, that plan being to move toward Stevenville, just west of Black Creek. This placed the Fenians in the center of a triangle, with Peacocke to the north, Booker closing in from the west and Dennis at Fort Erie to the southeast.

Dennis found only a few men left behind in Fort Erie and Frenchman's Creek. Booker loaded his men onto trains to Ridgeway for the march on to Stevenville. O'Neill was in place on Lime Ridge, waiting to engage and hoping to defeat the militia before they were joined by the British regulars. He was in a pincer and did not know it.

Ridgeway Awakens!

Only one horse came by train from Port Colborne, Booker's own horse. This meant that ammunition and supply wagons had to be sent back, since there were no horses available in Ridgeway. The soldiers had to draw enough rounds to keep themselves stocked; they had between forty to sixty rounds each on average. The Queen's Own Rifle Company No. 5 took the forefront of Booker's column. When they stepped off the train, every man had a loaded weapon. When they arrived at Lime Ridge, they had already marched a mile along one of the roadways. Now they came face to face with the Fenians, who opened fire, with the Queen's Own No. 5 receiving the first volley. Reports say this battle began with shots fired at seven thirty in the morning. Canadian/British forces advanced until they came to the Fenian bullet screen. Nobody can agree on how long they were thus engaged; some say thirty minutes, while others say three hours. Whatever the case, the Fenians were forced to fall back.

The Fenians were now in a battle with almost one thousand, minus the eighty men Dennis had taken to Fort Erie. They were greatly outnumbered, but another of those surprising events that sometimes turn the tides of battle was about to occur.

O'Neill's men had managed to procure some horses, so there were mounted men among them, whereas their opponents had only Booker's horse and no others. Canadian stories say that the bugle calls Booker used to signal his men during the battle were somewhat confusing, and seeing the Fenians on horseback, the call turned to one of resisting the cavalry. Because of this, Canadian forces withdrew from the press against the Fenians. The

Irishmen gained some much-needed breathing room, while the Canadians took formations to oppose a cavalry charge. As a result, when the folly of this information became known, British officers attempted to break these formations. In doing so, several men were crushed and trampled by charging Fenians and Canadians, who now pushed into them again. This confusion allowed the Fenians to once more gain the upper hand, with the Canadians falling back. Fenian losses on the ridge are unknown, but the Queen's Own lost nine men, and forty others were wounded.

The Fenians won this brief encounter as the Canadians dispersed back to meet the train. A Ridgeway doctor named Brewster kept an account of what he saw that day and wrote that there was much chaos, with wagons full of civilians coming in to take a look, much like the events at Bull Run, and soon after, soldiers and officers running back the other way. He further stated that the Canadian militia was not battle seasoned and had no leadership to help it hold its position once the Fenians had it on the run. The Fenians took Dr. Brewster prisoner, and upon seeing their United States uniforms, he expressed appall at their use. He himself had served in the Union army during the Civil War and felt they sullied the uniform with an unjust cause not supported by the country to which they belonged.

The village of Ridgeway was now in Fenian hands, and here they rested, some in the doctor's own house. Brewster would also later recount that the number of mounted men among the Fenians was probably no more than two or three and not cavalry at all. The luck of the Irish!

We are the Fenian Brotherhood,
Skilled in the Arts of war.
And we're going to fight for Ireland,
The land that we adore,
Many battles we have won,
Along with the boys in blue,
And we'll go and capture Canada
For we've nothing else to do.

The Fenians set up an earthworks on the ridge, and later, on June 2, after having rested and taken a few souvenirs, O'Neill's men were divided in two. He led some back to Fort Erie, and Starr did the same, but in a different direction. O'Neill could not be certain of the whereabouts of the remaining Canadian forces, and by dividing his men, he covered more ground; unfortunately, he also dwindled their firepower. O'Neill was met by Dennis and his men onboard a tug when he marched into the village of Fort Erie. This was at approximately four o'clock in the afternoon. The tug held fifty-eight captives from O'Neill's army.

In seconds, an exchange of fire rang out. A cheer rose up from the U.S. shore, where thousands of spectators had gathered. The tug, with its prisoners, pulled out into the river, and the Fenians rallied against the militia. Half this Canadian force took refuge in the Lewis House, and the rest retreated north. There were heavy casualties in both battles of the day. Colonel Dennis succeeded in making good an escape, disguising himself and hiding in a village residence until it was safe on the morning of June 3. He then ran to make his report to Peacocke.

Although O'Neill had mastered his army of Irish Americans and stood on Canadian soil currently victorious, he knew he had no hope of continuing

Battle of Ridgeway. *Courtesy of the Library of Congress Print and Photographs Division.*

further. He had defeated eighty British and Canadian troops with his nearly eight hundred men, but there would be no reinforcements for the remainder of the plan. The *Michigan* and its patrol boats blocked his retreat to the States, and there was still a Canadian British threat to be reckoned with. Resigned to this fact, any enemy prisoners he had were released, and he withdrew his troops to Old Fort Erie, where he vowed to make a final stand for the cause. Even though he was given word that Fenians and weapons were about to cross from Buffalo to his aid, he was resolved. His day had come and gone, and there was no way to win. Nevertheless, he felt he had done a great service to Ireland, as he had drawn attention there away from St. Lawrence, as had been the plan all along. Perhaps the entire cause was not lost.

In the predawn hours of June 3, John O'Neill and his men left the Canadian shores on canalboats that had been sent to meet them. As the boats neared the middle of the river, the delineation mark between the borders, an armed tug under command of the *Michigan* fired a warning shot across their path. O'Neill's immediate surrender was demanded, and in the end, he felt it was best to take his chances with the *Michigan* and the United States rather than to be overrun and his men captured or killed on foreign soil. O'Neill made the right decision. By noon that day, Fort Erie was taken over by the British and Canadian militia. Most of O'Neill's men were held aboard the scow *A.P. Waite*, which was tied to the *Michigan*. They were guarded by reinforcements from Fort Porter.

Tramp, tramp, tramp, the boys are marching,
Cheer up, let the rabble come!
For beneath the Union Jack,
we'll drive the Fenians back
And we'll fight for our beloved Canadian home.
Cheer up boys, come on, come on!
It will not take us long
To prove to their dismay,
That their raid will not pay
And wish that from Canadian ground
They stayed away.

On June 4, the prisoners were shipped via train to Toronto to stand trial. Paraded through the city streets to the jail, the Fenians were chastised by the citizens with garbage, debris and words. Officers were released two days later with the promise to appear before the Federal Circuit Court at Canandaigua, New York. The remaining Fenian prisoners were put on trial in Toronto, and of those, seven were sentenced to hanging, a Roman Catholic priest among them. None of these sentences was carried out. Instead, the prisoners were paroled and sent by train back to their homes in the United States, charged never again to cross international borders.

The commanders who led the defense in Canada were found to be incompetent and in dereliction of duty. John O'Neill was promoted to general in the Fenian Brotherhood and went on to become Fenian president, leading two other raids, both of which were thwarted by a now prepared Canadian defense force. No charges were brought against the Fenians at Canandaigua, furthering the conjecture that perhaps the United States appreciated the idea of Canada being seized. In fact, in December of that same year, all weapons seized by the *Michigan* were returned to O'Neill's men.

General Tom Sweeny said, "If I had done this in another country, I would be a hero. But here, here I am just one of the boys, prowling the night with the other highwaymen."

Whether you view the incident as a raid or invasion would largely depend on whether you sided with the Irish or Canadians. Either way, brave men died on both sides, an international incident was averted and a truly remarkable, if somewhat wicked, event took its place in local history. If not for British spies and the lack of reinforcements, we might be calling Canada the United Irish Republic.

On July 4, 1866, Fenian President Robert gave an address in Buffalo, as recorded in the *New York Times*. The following portions of his speech show clearly how the Fenians viewed their place in history and explain why reinforcements did not reach O'Neill in Canada:

> *If it had not been for the measures of the Washington Cabinet, there is no question but that we would be in quiet possession of every foot of English territory on this Continent, and shown such an example to the oppressed nationalities of the earth, and made such a glorious record in history that our names would descend to countless generations yet unborn, and our accomplishment descend in history as the most brilliant ever recorded.*

...Our men were stopped from going on the railroads; the telegraph offices were not permitted to send the businesses dispatches of any kind until they had been to Washington, and nothing was permitted to come from the front unless it contained bad news. Anything that was bad or a request to recall our men from Canada was allowed to come at once, but I made up my mind I would not call them back until I saw it was impossible to reinforce them. I had means to send more arms and ammunition, but found that was stopped by a general order from the Government to the Railroad Companies not to allow men suspected of being Fenians to pass; not to take freight suspected of containing arms and ammunition, on the pain of having their business broken up. And then there were the secret orders to the

William R. Robert, president of the Fenian Brotherhood. *Courtesy of the Library of Congress Print and Photographs Division.*

> *different officials to crush them out by every means. Meade went gathering them up at the railroad depots, forcing them to go home.*

In his address, Robert continued to explain the ways in which the United States government worked behind the scenes to foil the Fenians' plans and claimed that as citizens of the United States, the Fenians were treated unjustly under the rights given to citizens to travel and correspond freely.

Throughout the movement, the Fenians had a countersign in order to recognize one another as friends. According to Robert, it was "Erin go bragh." And who would deny that! Yet this wasn't the first time the Irish banded together for a cause in the region.

Prior to the 1863 strike riots in Buffalo and the Fenian fiasco of 1866, Irish canal workers were involved in two other notable confrontations in Lockport, New York. The first was on Christmas Eve 1822, when fighting broke out between Irish workers and the men of the town. John Jennings was killed, and this led to Lockport's first trial. Then, in the fall of 1823, the Irish became embroiled in a slave-hunting incident.

Standing Up Against Slavery

Joseph Pickard was a barber who had settled in Lockport, New York, after fleeing from his master in Kentucky. The Fugitive Slave Act of 1793 was old, but it was still enforceable and had not yet been replaced by the 1850 act. One should note that both did nothing to help the fugitives and everything to help slave owners. The 1850 Fugitive Act was to placate Southern slave owners and was part of the pre–Civil War Compromise of 1850. The Act of 1793 was designed to protect slave owners' property rights and stated that the government could pursue runaway slaves in any state or territory. It did, however, afford the slave a hearing in front of a judge.

Two slave hunters from Kentucky traveled to Western New York with the sole purpose of returning Joseph to his owner. However, Joseph had become a part of the Lockport community, and nothing irked a Northerner more than a Southerner attempting to take away someone's freedom or an outsider telling him what to do. Truth be told, the Southerners didn't much like that either. Not to mention the fact that Western New York had a large

Slaves were smuggled into and out of the Niagara Region. The "contraband" *schottische. Courtesy of the Library of Congress Print and Photographs Division.*

Quaker community by that time, and the Quakers upheld personal freedom and detested slavery. They were responsible for assisting many runaways in their flight to freedom.

Joseph had his day in court, but frightened and having tasted freedom, he jumped from the courthouse window and attempted to flee. A large crowd of Irishmen and others under the employ of two Quaker brothers, Joseph and Darius Comstock, had filled the street outside the building. Joseph apparently leapt in the midst of them when he jumped, and the Irish, understanding the desire to be free, took a stand to help in his escape. The slave hunters were in hot pursuit with pistols, but this didn't thwart the workers as they tried to block the way. The scuffle was short, and Joseph was returned to the courthouse.

Did they take him back to Kentucky? No. The Fugitive Slave Act did have one piece in it that spoke in his favor. A man had to be able to prove that a slave belonged to him. While the slavers had a warrant under the law for his arrest, they had no proof of ownership. Joseph Pickard was released.

Fifteen Miles on the Erie Canal

No story of the region would be complete without including an overview of life on the Erie Canal, since it really transformed this region out of the wilderness. Nor can stories be told without including the Irish, who were practically the sole workforce on the canal. They were often called "bogtrotters" since they worked long days under swampy, boggy, mosquito-infested conditions to build the world's longest canal. They worked twenty-eight days out of the month for between eight and ten dollars per month—just pennies a day. Of course, they were given an allotment of whiskey as well.

Fifteen miles was just about the distance a mule could pull a canalboat before having to be relieved by a new team, but some say it was also the distance at which kegs of whiskey were buried to encourage the diggers to work. Other stories say barrels were placed at intervals of less than fifteen miles and that was how the diggers got their pay. These may be no more than jabs at the Irish, but one thing we do know is that the Irish gave us the first canal songs. Written over their favorite tunes from home, these songs have settled into our folklore, as have the memories of an age that was both filled with adventure and fraught with danger.

I've got a mule and her name is Sal,
Fifteen miles on the Erie Canal,
She's a good old worker and a good old pal,
Fifteen miles on the Erie Canal.

We've hauled some barges in our day,
Filled with lumber, coal and hay,
And we know every inch of the way,
From Albany to Buffalo.

The first locks in Lockport were multi-stepped, as seen in this view of the upper village of Lockport. *Courtesy of the Library of Congress Print and Photographs Division.*

Low Bridge, everybody down,
Low Bridge for we're coming to a town,
And you always know your neighbor,
You always know your pal,
If you ever navigated on the Erie Canal.

The men who dug and were paid mere pennies often had to sleep in one room, and the cost of room and board could be as much as they made in a month. Dirty, loud and bug-ridden, it's hard to imagine that their temperaments were much improved by the loss of sleep. But it wasn't just the men working on the canals who had difficult lives. The canawlers who ran the boats that carried goods often traveled with their families. These boats had very little room for living with so much space devoted to cargo, and very little could be carried on top of these squatty vessels, as the bridges were low in many places to help save money. Anyone or anything sitting on top of a boat that didn't heed the warning "Low Bridge!" would be toppled off into the muddy water. In some cases, they might be in danger of being crushed by the boat itself. It was reported that one woman, on a passenger boat, fell asleep atop the boat with her head on a box, and her head was crushed by a bridge. Others made a game of dodging the bridge by mimicking the call with variations like "All Jackson men bow down!" Some boatmen were known to wait until they approached a bridge and then would jump off the boat onto the bridge, run across to the other side and hop back on the boat again. The steersman was most susceptible to bridges from where he stood on the boat, as the following excerpt from "Boating on the Bullhead" eludes.

The next morning I was boosted
To the stern cabin's roof.
With the tiller there I roosted
And watched the driver hoof.

Now the boat she was a Bullhead
Decked up to the cabin's top.
Many canawlers now are dead
Who had no place to drop.

When the bowsman he forgot to yell
"Low bridge, duck 'er down."
The Bullhead steersman went to Hell
With a bridgestring for a crown.

We were loaded down with Star Brand salt
The Captain was loaded, too.
I wouldn't say it was all his fault
But what was a man to do?

The bridge was only a heave away
When I saw it 'round the bend.
To the Cap a word I didn't say
While tumbling end over end.

So canawlers take my warning
Never steer a Bullhead boat.

Or they'll find you some fair morning
In the E-ri-e afloat.

Do all your navigating
From a line barn filled with hay.
And low bridge you won't be hating
And you'll live 'til Judgment Day.

Getting wet wasn't so bad if you didn't get run over by the boat, but it was what the murky water might hold that scared most people. Some told stories of a serpent, much like the Loch Ness monster, that lived in the canal, but far worse than that was the debris. People living on the canal without indoor

Life on a canalboat. Women gather to share news onboard a barge. *Courtesy of the Library of Congress Print and Photographs Division.*

Raising a family on a canalboat was hard work. Children lived, learned and played onboard. *Courtesy of the Library of Congress Print and Photographs Division.*

plumbing used that water for everything conceivable, from bodily functions to washing clothes and bodies, to cooking and even drinking.

No wonder there was so much disease, dysentery, typhus and, later, cholera. In the spring, the canal had to be drained and cleaned, and they found everything in that muck, from garbage and refuse to dead mules, dogs, cats, fish and even people. Imagine raising your children under these conditions, without school and often in questionable company. These people were tough because they had to be.

Canal incidents ran the gamut from drowning to bridge accidents to automobiles ending up in the water.

RIVER DANCER MEETS THE BROCKPORT BRIDGE

The canal is a beautiful place today, although waters can still be stirred up by storms. Traveling for leisure on the Erie Canal is reminiscent of the stories of Tom Sawyer and Huck Finn. Boats move slowly, usually no more than ten miles per hour, past quaint villages and waving walkers and bicyclers who meander the footpaths set up by the State of New York. The bridges are higher, and in spots, the canal is wider than it used to be. This is the new Erie Canal, with its width expanded to take the larger barges and steam tugs of the 1900s. Boating under road bridges, one might see the boxes and blankets of the homeless too. They find shelter there and fish for what they eat, though eating the fish from the canal isn't really advisable.

The locks at Lockport are perhaps the largest this side of Albany. Once consisting of several narrow locks lifting and lowering boats on the same escarpment over which Niagara Falls tumbles, the modern lock is now two steps and wide enough for a dozen boats to enter at the same time if they line both walls.

One feels small and insignificant entering the gaping maw of the lock. The gate creaks open, a thundering boom sounds in the depths and you gaze up at twenty-five feet of steel. Then, once you have the hold ropes in hand, the gate closes with a loud metallic crash. The waters begin to boil up from beneath your boat, and you feel the awesome power of the hydraulics as they open so water can fill the lock chamber and raise you to the next level. The boat pulls away from the wall, and you hold on to the slimy rope with one hand. As the waters move, the boat is pushed hard against the wall, and you push off with the boat hook in your other hand. Your heart races as you watch the water level rise and see faces above come into view where spectators watch and wave. That fascination of an old way of life is still present. Now, the gate opens, and you enter the second lock and repeat it all again, but this time the ride seems easier. The gates clang open, and you are underway. The locks at Lockport are by far the most awe-inspiring and scariest of all. But the double bridges in some towns can be more hazardous.

In this computer age, it is interesting that the bridges still employ lift tenders. In towns where they have double bridges, such as Brockport, the tender works both. He lifts the bridge for a boat at one end and then, once the boat enters, he lowers it for road traffic to resume while the boat idles, holding position. The lift tender then drives his car a short distance to operate the second bridge. But turbulent water or strong winds can make it difficult to idle a larger boat, and a boat with a twin engine that relies on both engines to help it steer is in danger when only one engine is working. That's what happened to our 1957 Richardson cruiser *River Dancer* when it lost an engine between the Brockport bridges and quickly lost steerage.

The captain struggled with the single engine against high winds to keep the vessel straight, but the boat quickly neared the lowered second lift bridge. The captain called for the first mate (me) to push them off the bridge, and the first mate, with boat hook in hand, stood on the boat's narrow toe rail doing just that until the bridge was just six inches from her nose. The boat now turned sidewise against the lowered bridge and was caught under the roof of the cockpit. At the same time, the lift tender finally arrived, raced up the stairs of his control tower and began raising the bridge. The boat was suddenly pulled out of the water to the loud sound of tearing and crushing as the canvas covering the cockpit was torn away and the overhead ripped apart. When the lift tender saw this, he immediately began lowering the bridge again. The captain, also having seen this, was doing his best to free the boat, but now the wind pushed the cruiser bow-first toward the concrete walls. The first mate carefully but swiftly made her way to the bow to push the *River Dancer* off the wall, and the boat swung backward under a now raised bridge toward rocks on the other side. But this time, the skipper, a well-seasoned and experienced captain, was able to use the troublesome wind to his advantage. He brought the boat under control and regained steerage, thus avoiding the rocks along the embankment. The boat limped on down the canal to the first port it found and there underwent some repairs. The crew underwent some much-needed rest. Such accidents are not uncommon, and not even the mules, with their sure footing, were immune to danger in earlier days.

One of the most important workers on the canal was the mule. Teams towed the packet boats by way of the towpaths with lines that stretched from the mules to the boats. Every now and then there would be a board stretched over a large hole in the towpath. Now, mules are sure-footed, but they are also cantankerous. They sometimes balked at the orders given and fell into the canal. The walls of the canal made it impossible for the animals to gain footing on land, so one of the hoggee's jobs was to help pull the mule out by getting it near one of these holes where it could be coaxed to walk up a ramp out of the water. Sadly, many mules did not survive their swim and were found only when the canal was drained for cleaning. Hoggees (perhaps from "haw gee," a cry made to getup the mule) were the drivers who encouraged the teams along the path, cared for the animals, cleaned up after them and even slept with them. Sometimes the hoggees were young boys.

While an important job, apparently the hoggees received a fair amount of teasing from other workers, whose jobs were less involved with the hard and sometimes smelly business of mule driving.

Hoggee on the towpath 5 cents a day,
picking up the mule balls to eat along the way,
Hoggee on the towpath don't know what to say,
Walk behind a mules behind, all the live long day.

FROM ITALY WITH LOVE

As with other European countries, crop failure and famine struck Italy, forcing many to seek a life elsewhere. By the mid-1800s, a large wave of Italian immigrants, ten thousand or more, had settled on Buffalo's west side in the Canal District. Little Italy, or Dante Place, reflected this new settlement. Of all the immigrant communities in the region, theirs was the one that kept most to itself, with little interaction beyond neighborhood borders. This helped their culture to thrive but also kept them segregated. The bad reputation of the former Canal Street district may be one reason they were kept out of the mainstream when it came to representation in the legal and political systems.

Poor but hardworking, these new residents of the city often took the work nobody else wanted, and even the children needed to help support their families—or at least as much as the child labor laws would allow. Most children were able to work after age thirteen, and many quit school in order to do so. Perhaps because so many of the new Italian American residents had fled drought and famine and had been farmers, much of the Italian labor force employed in the region was in outdoor work. A few did manage to make good with their own businesses, yet these new Italian owned and operated businesses mostly served Little Italy. Few became successful outside the community. However, the Italian community had great success and good media representation when it supplied much of the construction, stonework and entertainment for the Pan-American Exposition, which opened in Buffalo in May 1901.

Immigration to a new country was always risky. Often, a male family member would come at the call of another already established here and gain roots before sending for the remainder of the family to join him. Sometimes the sponsor of this individual would be a padrone, a patron who set up living space and work in advance for these immigrants. These padrones were not always the most honest resources, but for many they were the only ones. They set high fees in exchange for their services, and unless immigrants already had family living here, what choice did they have but to pay it? When they did accept a padrone's assistance, there was no guarantee of permanent work. Very often, it was temporary at best, but now that the immigrant was here in this new land, he had to forge forward on his own. Not the best of situations for anyone. Yet fate has a way of working its

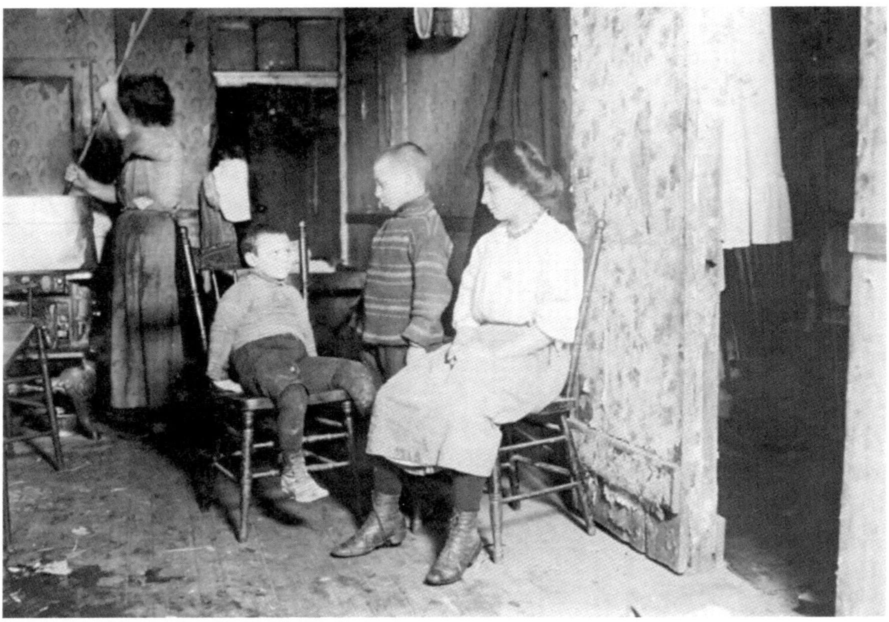

Paresse family, 4 Fly Street. Many Italian families worked in the Albion Canning Factory. *Courtesy of the Library of Congress Print and Photographs Division.*

The two children and their mother made seventy cents per day. *Courtesy of the Library of Congress Print and Photographs Division.*

magic on the downtrodden, and these young men often found work on their own, opening small businesses that occasionally thrived and went on to be major influences in their community. They worked in grocery, pasta, music, barbershop, shoemaking and restaurant businesses.

The family was all-important in Italian society. Women stayed home to raise the children. Religious and societal beliefs kept marriages together even during hardships. The only exception to women staying home was during harvest season, when whole families were known to work in local fields and canneries. Everyone pulled their weight for the family.

There was a lot of prejudice in the period when these immigrants arrived. Ironically, the immigrants were needed to feed the increasing workforce but were also despised because of it. They took work, they worked hard and this sometimes made others jealous. Their insulated community did not help change these prejudices. Notwithstanding, the Italian community also followed territorial boundaries of their homeland, with five distinct colonies separated by homeland cultural differences. There were districts within the overall Italian community for those from Campobasso, Calabria, Campagna, Abruzzi and Sicily. The latter took over the Hooks, also called Canal Street.

Nine- and twelve-year-old Italian newsies selling after school in Buffalo, New York. *Courtesy of the Library of Congress Print and Photographs Division.*

Strong bonds remained between these new Italian American settlers and families in the old country. It was a metaphorical chain that reached from here to across the ocean. In many ways, whole sections of Italian communities were set down right in Buffalo, with multiple generations living side by side. The streets around these homes became extensions of their living quarters and their families, making them self-sustaining territories.

The Italian communities were not particularly fond of outsiders either. Their numbers had pushed Irish settlement away from the waterfront, and the Irish sometimes pushed back. Fights were often bloody and involved knife play rather than the fisticuffs the Irish were used to. With so many people living so close together, and not under the best of circumstances, violence remained part of the culture of the street—a kickback to the earlier canal days—even though the district had become more family oriented.

NEW BUSINESS

The influx of immigration into the United States from so many European countries brought immigrants for many reasons. They wanted to make a better life for themselves; some were indentured, some were desperate for work and some fled trouble in the Old Country. This trouble included legal problems, revolutions, wars, famine and sometimes rivalries.

Work was plentiful in the United States during the industrial revolution. Many really believed the streets were "paved with gold" and only wished to pick that gold up and line their pockets with it. Whatever their reasons for coming, the cities quickly became populated and crammed with people who followed dreams, but some met nightmares in the tenements and sweatshops that abounded. The Niagara Region, with its hydroelectric power, led the way in New York State industry, making Buffalo the second largest city in the state and among the largest in the country. This city became home to many new immigrants, and the population doubled, tripled and quadrupled in a very short time.

But not all immigrants have had good intentions, and not all businesses have been legitimate. An easy fix for many was the route of organized crime, and some brought these roots with them. Mobsters of the twentieth century kept the police and FBI busy, while helping many politicians reach the top of their game. They offered protection to businesses and neighborhoods, but at a cost. The Niagara Region played a large role in this "new business" of crime, from Buffalo to Niagara Falls and into Canada. After all, the waterways and border were perfect for smuggling during Prohibition. The roots of the Mafia are undeniably Italian—in particular, Sicilian—and larger families still exist today, although not as strong in the Niagara Region. A major national "bust" on January 20, 2011, netted over one hundred Mafia members, some from New York State.

The FBI currently estimates that 25,000 Mafia members are active within the United States, with over 250,000 worldwide. American groups still include the Sicilian Mafia, the Camorra (gang) or Neapolitan Mafia (Naples), the Calabrian and the United Sacred Crown. These groups are scattered throughout the country, but New York State is among the four most active states. These organizations focus mainly on drug trafficking and money laundering but have also dealt in illegal gambling, political corruption, prostitution, murder, bombings and weapons dealing. The members arrested in January 2011 had colorful names reminiscent of those from the mob's earliest roots. Names swept up in this bust included Vinny Carwash, Baby Shacks, Tony Bagels, Junior Lollipops, Baby Fat Larry and others. The Niagara Region was once home to some of the Mafia's most notorious bosses, including Don Stefano, also called "Big Steve the Undertaker," and his Buffalo family known as "the Arm."

The Mafia was originally formed in Sicily in the 1800s as a means of defending the peasants against their enemies during an invasion by the French and the Arabs. The word Mafia is said to come from two sources, the Arab word for "Refuge" and an Italian acronym for "Morte Ala Franceise Italia Annela" or "Death to French is Italy's Cry." To be a member of the mafia was to be a "Man of Honor" and respected for taking care of family.

Many members fled Italy in the 1900s, when Benito Mussolini tried to destroy the Italian Mafia, including the Sicilian Mafia. They immigrated illegally into the United States, where they established La Costa Nostra, sometimes translated as "This Thing of Ours." To be a member of the Mafia was considered an honor. In fact, members of the Cosa Nostra

Getaway car—a 1930 Plymouth. *Courtesy of the author.*

adhered to a code call Omerta, which means "Code of Silence." When they swore this oath, they put the Mafia family above their own and agreed to remain silent and not to strike another "family" member, which would be considered a strike on the boss himself. To break Omerta was punishable by death.

The Roaring Twenties ushered in the high-water mark for the Mafia in America. The Mafia ran the cities by owning the police and the politicians. It thrived through gambling and prostitution, but the ratification of the Eighteenth Amendment to the United States Constitution on January 16, 1919, catapulted it to its greatest power. This was the beginning of Prohibition:

> *No person shall on or after the date when the 18th Amendment to the Constitution of the United States goes into effect, manufacture, sell, barter, transport, import, export, deliver, furnish or possess any intoxicating liquor except as authorized in this act.*

Some believe Prohibition was the United States government's biggest mistake as it helped fertilize the roots of organized crime.

Password: "Joe Sent Me"

Prohibition brought about the rise of speakeasies in America. Lawmakers, under pressure from temperance organizers, made the laws they believed would make the country stronger, but instead they only made Americans more eager to find a drink and crime organizations stronger through the sale of illegal liquor. Drinking became a game of cat and mouse. Previously, women had not been allowed in bars, but now with underground and secret drinking establishments, they partook as equals to the men. Both hard liquor and the beer brewing industry took a hit.

By the mid-1800s, German's made up at least one-third of Buffalo's population. At first, many came to America fleeing difficult political and religious situations in Germany, but by the time of the industrial revolution, they were coming for work like so many others. Following World War I, German immigration to the United States decreased dramatically. Laws prohibited them from coming. Yet German contributions to the city of Buffalo and the

Niagara Region—in fact, to the entire country—cannot be ignored. Already highly skilled when they entered the country, Germans settling in Buffalo were shoemakers, stoneworkers, clock makers and well educated men. Indeed, they could create things that were needed by a burgeoning city. They opened banks and had a hospital, and many were skilled brewers. Germans owned the most prominent breweries and department stores in Buffalo, and unlike other ethnic groups that settled here, their influence was felt outside their community. Jacob Schoellkphf founded the first electric power company here, and by the late 1800s, his tanning and flourmills were among the largest in the entire country.

There were over thirty breweries in Buffalo by the late nineteenth century, many German owned and operated. Beer was an important commodity, as Buffalo was an industrial city with a large German population. Much of the beer was consumed locally—some say 100 million barrels per year—while the rest was sold elsewhere. Breweries and saloons had a symbiotic relationship; they relied on one another for survival. In fact, the breweries owned many saloons. These breweries included names that many Americans have long forgotten: Simon Pure, Iroquois, Schieber, Gerhard Lang and

Bottles and a barrel of confiscated whiskey. *Courtesy of the Library of Congress Print and Photographs Division.*

Phoenix. With the Eighteenth Amendment, most of these breweries and others across the country were forced to sell soda pop or close their doors forever. Very few survived. But many saloons managed to keep going. They offered meals and a place to gather, and some had backroom speakeasies—or as one might say, "social clubs."

Ask the bartender for a drink, and he was liable to whisper, "Speak easy, friend." This is how the term speakeasy came into popular use during the Roaring Twenties. The average person, J.Q. Public, went to his local gin joint, blind pig or blind tiger, as they were sometimes called. These terms supposedly came from the owner of an establishment charging the patron to see something interesting, like a strange animal, and then they received a "complimentary" beverage. Higher-class patrons frequented the speakeasies, however, and needed either a membership card or a password to enter. Unlike the blind pigs, a speakeasy touted the best bootleg liquor with dining and entertainment and required its patrons to be dressed in appropriate eveningwear. The Mafia operated many of these speakeasies, and the Niagara Region was not immune to organized crime and everything that went with it. In fact, it became a crucial location. During Prohibition, some say Buffalo had as many as eight thousand speakeasies.

One such pub, sadly torn down in 2008 because the owner did not keep the property in safe condition, was McBride's Pub on Chicago Street in Buffalo's old first ward. This hotel and pub, once named Kitty O'Malley's, is said to have been the place where the Fenian Brotherhood met to plan its invasion into Canada, as well as the location, known as Quinn's in 1913, used to plan the city's first Saint Patrick's Day Parade. As McBride's, it was reportedly a speakeasy in the 1920s.

There was also the Rose Garden Restaurant in Lancaster, New York. Jenny Morris operated it as a speakeasy until her arrest. Later, it became a popular German eatery and beer garden and is still in operation as a restaurant today. One of the best-known current eateries, Ulrich's Pub on Ellicott Street, has been under operation for over one hundred years. Ulrich's was at one time owned by one of two breweries consecutively, Weyand's and Phoenix. They controlled the pub until 1910. It also became a speakeasy.

When the government increased the cost of liquor licenses in 1890, many small saloons went out of business. They could not pay the exorbitant fees. But the breweries had the money, and their saloons thrived, giving them a certain amount of power over small "corner establishments." At one time, there was a tavern on almost three out of four corners in every part of the city, and each sold the brew made by its owner. In 1896, the Raines law caused further problems for these saloons. That law said that only hotels serving food could operate on Sunday, a major day the working man could frequent the saloons, and many of those were owned by Germans who gathered there on the day of rest. But rather than fold, these business-minded Germans renamed their saloons, calling them hotels and served a small menu of food. The free lunch became another way to serve alcohol, as long as you ordered liquor, you didn't pay for the meal. Where there's a will, there's a way, which brings us to the speakeasy and the bootleg industry. Remember, liquor was legal in Canada, and Canada is literally a stone's throw across the Niagara River from Buffalo. These were the days of the rumrunners, who smuggled liquor across the border and into city establishments.

Beer is not as easy to make as liquor, so it was not as prevalent as bootleg whiskey during Prohibition. The term bootleg comes from the act of hiding a flask in one's knee-high boot and dates to the early days of the settlers, when traders, trappers, cowboys and Indians reportedly did just that. This bootleg liquor, whiskey or beer was not the same quality as that made by professional brewers. Sometimes people made it for their own consumption and sometimes to bottle and sell illegally. Many times, it was made in a bathtub, hence the term bathtub gin.

Bootleg whiskey was all that was available after personal reserves were depleted, and it could be deadly. Many people died, and the lucky ones went blind—if you can call that lucky. The beer that was produced in small quantities was often called "alley" beer, as it was made in secret warehouse operations. When it had a very small alcoholic content, it was sometimes called "near" beer.

Even with its apparent dangers, the tradition of the speakeasy continued right up until the Eighteenth Amendment was repealed in December 1933. When Prohibition ended, thousands of breweries in the United States had been depleted to half the number, and of Buffalo's thirty breweries, only seven remained. These converted to selling mostly beer in the bottle rather than on draft, as has been the tradition prior to Prohibition. After all, their breweries had switched to making bottled soda pop. It wasn't cost effective to convert back again. It was some time before draft beer served from the keg was readily available again.

CHEESE-IT! IT'S THE COPS!

The FBI and local police had their hands full with crime even before the new business of smuggling, bootlegging and illegal consumption of alcohol. Many raids attempted to put the speakeasies and blind pigs out of business, but as soon as one was shut down, it seemed another opened and operators were back in business.

Anticipating such raids, club owners came up with clever devices to dump the liquor and conceal the premises. Secret doors, drop shelves and hidden rooms abounded. And there were crooked policemen and politicians staging raids while taking handouts on the side to reopen the establishment as soon as nobody was looking. Hot jazz poured into the night; fast women and open pockets spilled the loot, and they danced the Charleston. What had been legal now entered the shadows and became a whispered tale. The crime bosses, mostly Mafia affiliated, grew more powerful than ever before, taking over as the middlemen between reluctant brewers, bootleggers and tavern owners. They became "untouchable."

Buffalo native district attorney William J. Donovan was the man Franklin D. Roosevelt entrusted with designing a plan for national security. This plan became the Central Intelligence Agency, or CIA.

Born into an illiterate working-class Irish family, William Donovan was raised on the belief that education was important. His parents insisted that he and his siblings learn to read, and they attended parochial schools. William, the oldest, attended law school and failed, but rumor has it that the dean of the school, future Supreme Court justice Harlan Stone, kept him from being expelled. William entered private practice in Buffalo, going on to become one of the country's most prominent lawyers, not to mention a respected citizen in the city of Buffalo and the Niagara Region.

Donovan's wartime heroics won him the nickname "Wild Bill." At the onset of World War I, he helped give aid to starving Europeans in neutral countries and later served as a battalion leader in New York's Sixty-ninth

Infantry Regiment. Donovan received a promotion to colonel and eventually to major general. He was awarded the Medal of Honor, the Distinguished Service Cross, the Distinguished Service Medal, two Purple Hearts and the Freedom Award. In 1941, Donovan would be named coordinator of information for the OSS (Office of Strategic Services), where he further distinguished himself. This was the organization that became the CIA.

Of course, Donovan's career wasn't hurt by marrying Ruth Rumsey, from one of the wealthiest families in Buffalo. He traveled a long way from Buffalo's First Ward to the upper class, but his bids for lieutenant governor in 1922 and later for governor of New York State in 1939 were crushed. His loss of the governorship is attributed to trifling with those who wished not to be trifled with during Prohibition, namely important Western New York voters. His loss was very likely a payback.

William J. Donovan, half-length portrait (standing, facing left). *Courtesy of the Library of Congress Print and Photographs Division.*

Tragically, William also later lost one of his two children in an automobile accident, his granddaughter to an incident of accidental poisoning and his wife to a drug and alcohol overdose in 1955. His own life and standing in Buffalo society was forever changed by his actions in the 1920s.

Donovan made many enemies when he raided some of Buffalo's most elite speakeasies and still more in the political arena when he refused to press charges. Furthermore, his career never went farther than assistant to the United States attorney general. He was Irish Catholic, and there were many who did not want "that" in a place of power. It was also rumored that he had been considered to run as Herbert Hoover's vice president, but for the same reason, he was crossed off the list.

Buffalo's mayor from 1922 to 1929 was Francis X. Schwab, who also happened to be part owner in the Broadway Brewing Company. Many feel this was his motivation for fighting against Prohibition. However, Schwab claimed it was because so many of his citizens were getting sick, going blind and dying from bad bootleg liquor. Whichever is true, he undeniably took the government to task on the issue and insisted on repeal. Mayor Schwab felt the speakeasies should be legalized and taxed in order to control them. He was opposed to Prohibition, but as mayor, he had to uphold the law. Like Donovan, he made some powerful enemies.

Also Catholic, Schwab went head to head with the Ku Klux Klan. The KKK was on a campaign against the Catholics and saw the mayor's divided motivations as a means to target him. Furthermore, the KKK made Prohibition one of its major issues: the KKK was for it, and Schwab was not. The Klan supported Prohibition's strict enforcement and was known to burn saloons and intercept liquor shipments. Schwab made himself even more unpopular by sending spies into the midst of the Klan's local chapter and by displaying a list of Klan members' names publicly. The list was published as "Expose of Traitors: In the Interests of Jews, Catholics, Negroes and all Respecters of the American Principle of Civil and Religious Freedom." The KKK hired a hit on Mayor Schwab, but it failed. In the end, he eradicated the Klan's existence locally.

The mayor is said to have operated above the law himself. In 1922, the same year as his election, he was charged with violating Prohibition when he manufactured and sold beer at his brewery. District Attorney Donovan was the prosecutor on Schwab's case, and although he tried to throw the book at the city leader, Schwab got off with a $500 fine. Mayor Francis Schwab's brewery, as it turns out, was only making "near" beer.

After losing this case, District Attorney Donovan may have needed to save face among his peers, and this sent him on his way to becoming the most hated man in Western New York. The DA raided several elite social clubs, including ones of which Donovan himself was a member.

Social clubs, or gentlemen's clubs, were popular during the 1800s and into the 1900s. Many of these men-only organizations existed simply because men of the upper class wanted to play cards, smoke, drink and involve themselves in activities not permitted in their homes. During Prohibition, many of these clubs acted as speakeasies for their members.

The Saturn Club was started in Buffalo by a small group of young men in 1885 for the same reasons many clubs were formed, and its membership grew to over three hundred by the early 1900s. Club members originally met in one another's homes until finally, in 1922, the club had a permanent location designed by architect Duane Lyman. Supposedly, this was the club Donovan was a member of, and in 1923, both the Saturn Club and the Buffalo Country Club were raided for breaking Prohibition. If the stories are true, the bartender was arrested, and illegal liquor was found in the lockers of many prominent citizens.

The Saturn Club motto at its inception was: "Where the women cease from troubling, and the wicked are at rest."

William Donovan died in February 1959, the only American to have received all four of the military's highest awards. Mayor Francis Schwab died in 1946. Both contributed to the stories of the Niagara Region.

Forget About It

The Italian Mafia was born in the nineteenth century. It was based on a clan system, with each clan controlling a territory. These territories were villages, towns or neighborhoods, and the business of these clans was protection, arms sales, smuggling, loan sharking, money laundering and political corruption. A flood of emigration from Italy in the late nineteenth-century into America planted seeds of those clans here. Though not directly tied to the Italian families, the Mafia of the United States operated on some of the same principles. With new leadership and time, the American Mafia grew to a new height, mostly due to the Eighteenth Amendment.

The Niagara Region, with its nearness to Canada, was once the territory of Big Steve the Undertaker and the Arm. Big Steve captained the helm of his family longer than any other boss in the country, from 1921 until about 1972.

Stefano Magaddino left his birthplace in Castellammare del Golfo Sicily and illegally entered the United States in about 1919 with one brother, Antonino. They first settled in New York City, where they worked in the bakery of an uncle, Vito Bonventre. Unlike the many immigrants who came here over the centuries, the brothers didn't come here for the golden-paved streets or because work was plentiful; they came to escape a rival gang in Italy, the Buccellato Clan.

Vito Bonventre, a baker by trade, was from the same Sicilian town as his nephew Stefano. He was also a mob boss and was tied to Magaddino's family for many years in the Old Country. His New York City bakery was a front business for his gang of hired assassins, the Good Killers. Vito knew that both Stefano and Antonino had talents with knives and guns, and it wasn't long before he had them under his wing. Stefano, along with another fellow Castellan, quickly moved up in the ranks.

The Good Killers' motto—"We will burn you"—came into use supposedly because a Bonventre rival who killed one of the clan was cut into pieces and burned in the bakery oven. But that was years before the Magaddinos arrived. The Good Killers' reach extended far, and they racked up murders throughout New York, Detroit, Pittsburgh and elsewhere.

While not named directly, Stefano Magaddino was considered responsible for the deaths of the Giannola brothers, Salvatore and Antonio, known as the wealthiest Italians in Detroit, and later, the death of John Vitale, also of Detroit and a serious rival of the Giannolas.

BLOOD FEUDS

Two households, both alike in dignity,
In fair Verona, where we lay our scene,
From ancient grudge break to new mutiny,
Where civil blood makes civil hands unclean.

From forth the fatal loins of these two foes
A pair of star-cross'd lovers take their life;
Whole misadventured piteous overthrows
Do with their death bury their parents' strife.
The fearful passage of their death-mark'd love,
And the continuance of their parents' rage,
Which, but their children's end, nought could remove,
Is now the two hours' traffic of our stage.

One needs only read William Shakespeare's *Romeo and Juliet* to know that rivalry and feuding are ancient. Perhaps it is more wicked that it continued in Italy and migrated to America and is still in many ways a part of those whispered tales. Although the feud of this story is not one of "star-crossed lovers," it is nonetheless tragic and bloody and gives insight into Stefano Magaddino's early history before moving to the Niagara Region, a history that no doubt made him who he was.

Stefano was born into a tradition. His father, Giovanni Magaddino, was Sicilian Mafia, a "man of honor." He built an alliance between his family and that of the Bonanno and Bonventre families. This alliance eventually led to a feud with another local family, the Buccelatos.

In 1899, a Buccellato murdered a Bonanno, so the Bonnanos and Magaddinos ordered hits on some of the Buccellatos. One can only guess how many people died as this fighting went back and forth, until finally they called a truce in 1905. That's a six-year feud! It was a peace that would not last.

During this period, many of the family members left Sicily for America, but Stefano Magaddino and his brothers, Antonino and Pietro, stayed behind. They continued to immerse themselves in the business of theft and extortion and learned to handle weapons. Since Stefano was born in 1891, that made him between the ages of fourteen and nineteen when he began his life of crime. Then, tragedy struck at Stefano's young heart. In 1910, the old feud was rekindled, and his brother, Pietro, was murdered. Many men were killed on both sides, and Stefano and Antonino were advised to leave, to go to Brooklyn, New York, in America to their uncle Vito.

But this feud did not remain in Sicily. Following the death of Pietro Magaddino, his killer or killers fled to the United States. A Buccellato man named Carmello Caizzo was fingered as having been the triggerman or at least one of those involved in the murder. He took up hiding in Avon, New Jersey. When Stefano learned of this, he set up the hit, but he couldn't act openly himself.

The Good Killers found a barber named Bartolo Fontana, who later confessed to the murder but said he had been forced into it. Fearing for his life, as he was privy to secretive information, Fontana snitched on the gang and turned himself in to the Italian Squad, an agency formed for dealing with the Italian Mafia in New York City.

Fontana was able to supply information to the authorities; he claimed that the Good Killers were forcing young immigrants into work under threats of extortion, torture and death. He further asserted that he had been one of these men forced to kill. But perhaps Bartolo had a more personal reason to rat out the gang: the man they made him kill, the man who had killed Magaddino's brother, was his best friend, Carmello Caizzo.

On August 19, 1921, the *New York Times* headline read, "125 Murders Now Charged to Band. Police Expect to Arrest Chief of the 'Good Killers' in Buffalo."

Several members of the Good Killers were arrested, including Vito Bonventre and Stefano Magaddino, but there was not enough supporting evidence to keep them imprisoned, and all were released—except, in a twist of irony, Fontana, who was sentenced. This might have been best for Fontana; after all, Stefano punched him openly in court and is said to have threatened him with the gang's motto: "I'm going to burn you."

The Buccellato Clan still had a few men in the city and put out a hit on Magaddino after his release. Stefano, with his friend and cohort Gaspar Milazzo, who would later become a prominent boss in Detroit, stepped from a shop on a New York City street. It only took a moment for them to recognize the familiar sound of screeching tires as a car whipped past with guns blazing. Two innocent bystanders were killed instantly, but the future big-time crime bosses escaped.

Stefano Magaddino then fled the Big Apple for the Niagara Region, where he joined the Buffalo gang of Guiseppe DiCarlo.

"The Chief"

Born in Vallelunga, Sicily, Guiseppe DiCarlo immigrated to the United States in 1908 and became a Buffalo, New York resident a short time later. He lived among the Castellans on Buffalo's west side and befriended Angelo "Buffalo Bill" Palmeri, the community boss. Palmeri was known to be a peaceful man, unwilling to get involved in rival gang wars. Over time, DiCarlo managed to unite the regional gangs and became head of the Buffalo crime ring, with Palmeri remaining in the background as his advisor.

It wasn't long before the twosome controlled the Italian district of Buffalo and labor on its waterfront. DiCarlo is named among the major leaders in the Good Killers; in fact, rumors abounded that DiCarlo was "the Chief" who controlled the gang, and this eventually brought him in contact with Stefano Magaddino. Buffalo police, questioned by local and national news organizations in 1921, denied any such Buffalo connection with the Mafia or with the Good Killers.

Palmeri maintained a saloon and, with DiCarlo, most likely made out very well when the government enacted Prohibition. Yet in 1919, Palmeri decided to retire to lead a growing Castellammare community in Niagara Falls. He left DiCarlo to run Buffalo. Guiseppe DiCarlo's reign over the Buffalo crime organization was short-lived. He died of natural causes in 1922, and his son, Joseph Jr., took over.

Don Stefano

Upon his arrival in Buffalo, it didn't take long for Stefano Magaddino to move up to a leadership position. Most likely, he had real family here as well, and before long, he was a major player in the region's underworld. Joseph DiCarlo and Magaddino had an unmistakable conflict of interests, and some stories say Magaddino's power overshadowed DiCarlo, who became an underboss. Magaddino kept Joseph DiCarlo on as underboss for many years, until in 1945, when he stripped DiCarlo of his duties—a smart move on Magaddino's part. DiCarlo had his own supporters, and this kept the peace between them, which helped give Don Stefano a firmer toehold.

Steve Magaddino at a crime hearing. *Courtesy of the Library of Congress Print and Photographs Division.*

Magaddino set up smuggling and bootlegging operations from Canada into the United States and maintained a Buffalo connection with the Brooklyn organization in New York City, where his cousin Joe Bonanno would become one of the youngest crime bosses in Mafia history. This contact gave Magaddino a seat on the Mafia Commission after it was formed in 1931.

Well liked within the American Mafia, Magaddino is said to have used as little violence as possible and managed his family carefully, thus furthering his lengthy control over them. It is difficult to believe that this would be the case with his years of experience, but in truth, few bosses acted on their own. Most just gave the orders, and that was usually done in secret.

Don Stefano ran the Niagara Region with enough business to keep his attention here until the end of Prohibition. When the Eighteenth Amendment was repealed, Magaddino's Arm turned to other means of support—loan sharking, gambling, drug trafficking and a menu of other illegal activities.

He expanded his empire to include Rochester and Ohio, as well as other locations, and this led to another assassination attempt on May 19, 1936.

Magaddino's brother-in-law, Nicholas Longo, and his sister, Arcangela, lived with their three daughters in a house next door to Stefano. A rival planted a bomb hoping to kill Magaddino, but it was planted in the wrong house. Instead of killing Magaddino, it was his sister who was killed. Her husband was apparently not home at the time, but their daughters were injured in the blast. Once more, tragedy hit close to Stefano's heart, but his life was filled with violence.

To maintain power meant that he had to be vigilant. It also meant that sometimes he had to cooperate, and cooperation usually led to more money for the family.

The Arm allowed Moe Dalitz "the Chinaman" and his "Little Jewish Navy," a Russian Jewish faction of Detroit's notorious Purple Gang, and the Cleveland Syndicate to smuggle Canadian whiskey from Niagara Falls, Canada, to Detroit and Cleveland. No doubt, Magaddino's Arm received a tribute for that generosity. However, when the Porrello family, the second leading Mafia in Cleveland, tried to get a piece of the action in Pennsylvania and Western New York, Magaddino forced them back to Cleveland with their tails tucked between their legs and the bodies to prove it—or so the tales are whispered.

By the time Magaddino finished building his crime empire, his Arm stretched from Buffalo and Niagara Falls to Rochester and Utica; parts of Pennsylvania; Youngstown, Ohio; and Canadian Niagara Falls, Hamilton and Toronto.

With ties to the Castellamarese in Brooklyn, when war broke out between the Castellamarese and a Manhattan gang, the Morello Gang, Magaddino is said to have helped fund them with cash each week, and when a leader from Chicago was targeted, it is believed Stefano brought him to Buffalo for protection. Unfortunately, this gang leader, Joe Aiello, did not heed the warnings and returned to Chicago only to be cut down by Al Capone, who supported the Morellos.

How else does Magaddino tie into this story? Besides helping with cash and hiding Aiello, when the head of the Morello Gang, Guiseppe Masseria (aka Joe "the boss" Masseria), was murdered in 1931, what came to be known as the Castellamarese War ended. Masseria's opposition, Maranzano, was in line to take over as official head of all five families in New York, but his luck changed when he was also killed by Masseria's slayer, "Lucky" Luciano. This put Magaddino's cousin Joseph Bonanno in the driver's seat as leader of the largest crime organization in the country.

Maranzano was slain in September 1931, and before year's end, the National Commission, a governing body for the Mafia in the United States, was created. Its core membership consisted of the bosses of the New York families, and one of those was Stefano Magaddino, "Big Steve the Undertaker."

Almost illiterate and unable to speak English when he entered the country, but already fluent in the language of crime, including murder, Magaddino became one of the American Mafia's most powerful bosses and helped set up one of the most famous (or infamous) Mafia meetings in U.S. history—the 1957 Apalachin Summit.

Apalachin Summit

While not held in the Niagara Region, the Apalachin Summit is significant to Magaddino's history. With a major seat on the commission, he was instrumental in decision-making and supposedly persuaded the commission to hold the meeting at the ranch of Joseph Barbara in Apalachin, New York. The New York underworld was experiencing so much infighting that it felt a meeting was needed to bring peace between the families. Staunch traditionalists, the old-timers were struggling to maintain a foothold over the newer, more liberal members. The Mafia was on the verge of an internal war. It was primarily a division in philosophy between Sicilian-born Mafia and Americanized Mafia—tradition versus profit. In the underworld, it was called "the cold war." Magaddino's place on the commission was one of only three remaining old guard seats. They were losing power, so Magaddino, always on top of his game and with his finger on the trigger, secretly sided with the new liberal faction.

The meeting took place on November 14, 1957, and nearly one hundred Mafia bosses and their retinues attended. Until that time, most authorities, including the FBI, had pretty much denied the existence of the Mafia. When so many expensive vehicles with out-of-town and out-of-state plates showed up in the small town, the police became suspicious. Police set up a roadblock. When a member of the meeting spotted the roadblock, he tipped

Following the failed Apalachin Summit and throughout Prohibition, police conducted raids on illicit establishments. *Courtesy of the Library of Congress Print and Photographs Division.*

off the attendees. Some fled by automobile and were netted; others tried to escape through fields. In the end, over fifty were detained, though not jailed, including Bonanno. Don Stefano was one of the bosses seen fleeing through a window. The Mafia was public. The FBI and President J. Edgar Hoover could no longer deny its existence.

Joseph Barbara, a major northeastern boss, lost face and power after the raid. What should have been an honor destroyed him. His home had been raided, and important Mafia figures were arrested there. This was a huge disgrace for him. What is most intriguing is that he was uneasy about the meeting being held there; he had said as much to Don Stefano. Even Bonanno had warned Stefano that it was a bad idea. But Stefano Magaddino, one of the most influential in choosing the site, ignored the warnings.

After that, most of the Mafia blamed Magaddino, and another attempt was made on his life at his home on Dana Drive in Lewiston, New York, in 1958. Someone tossed a grenade through his kitchen window. It failed to detonate.

Following the debacle at Apalachin, the Mafia was made public. Some members came forward and broke Omerta. This further lessened the power of the Mafia, even though few were prosecuted. Then, Joseph Profaci, one of the three traditionalists sitting on the commission, died of cancer in 1962, leaving only Bonanno and Magaddino. This placed them in a precarious position among their opposition, and in truth, there were plans to have Magaddino "removed."

Profaci was a friend of Bonanno, and another friend of his took the seat—Joe Magliocco. There was great turmoil within the organization, some of it secretive, some of it known. Betrayals, which were not necessarily commonplace with the old guard, brought forward information that Magliocco had put out a hit on prominent members, including Magaddino, and he had help with the plan from none other than Magaddino's own cousin, Bonanno. The commission called for the two "traitors to appear before it," but Bonnano refused. The commission booted him from his seat, yet Bonanno was stubborn in giving up his power.

Finally, in 1964, Magaddino's brother, Antonino, reportedly kidnapped Bonanno and held him for six weeks, just enough time for Bonanno's trusted capo and friend, Gaspar DiGregario, to be appointed head of the Bonanno family. Bonanno was already unpopular and was spending much of his time at his home in Arizona, yet he remained angry and steadfast in his desire to keep his power. This fueled what came to be known as the "Banana Split" or "Banana War." Eventually, Bonanno, powerless, went to Arizona permanently, leaving his New York business to others. A definite shift in power and procedure was in the wind. With Bonanno out of the way and all ties severed with him, Magaddino aligned himself with Johnny Papalia, aka "Pops."

The New Crew

John Papalia "owned" Hamilton, Ontario. He was born and bred there but was a Calabrian descendent. His claim to infamy was his heavy involvement in the French Connection, one of history's largest drug operations. The other was the Pizza Connection, and he was also involved in that.

Arrested in 1945 for the first time on burglary charges and again in 1947 for illegal gambling, "Pops" joined with a fellow inmate, who was already a well-established drug dealer in Toronto, Canada. After release from another arrest in 1949 for possession and selling heroine, for which he was acquitted, Papalia came in contact with a Bonanno associate in Canada who apparently tried to get him onboard with Bonanno's Canadian expansion. However,

Papalia chose to associate with Magaddino instead. After all, his father had been a bootlegger and was already in business with Don Stefano. By 1960, Papalia was a capo for Magaddino.

It was not long afterward that Papalia and the Agueci brothers, Vito and Alberto, began operating a branch of the French Connection from Canada into the United States. They did so with permission from Papalia's boss Magaddino and with help from the Buffalo Mafia. Some of the heroine was sold in Toronto and neighboring cities, but much had to be sold in the United States. The Papalia Agueci Group was under the direct protection of Magaddino, adding to the Arm's coffers. However, early 1961 spelled disaster for the Canadian trio.

Perhaps they just tried to get too big for their britches by bringing in too much heroine and pushing too many buttons, and they got into trouble with the law. Papalia was trying to get in on some gambling action in Toronto from Maxwell "Maxie Bluestein" Baker. When Baker wouldn't concede, Papalia and several of his goons severely beat Baker in a downtown Toronto tavern. Alberto was hauled in for carrying heroine and a baseball bat. Other members of their group were also nabbed and charged. Papalia and Agueci were extradited to the United States on drug charges. In 1964, Papalia was sentenced to ten years in the Lewisburg Federal Prison.

Alberto Agueci, according to some reports, believed he was to receive help from Buffalo in the way of bail if he was ever arrested, but soon after his arrest, he became aware of his "misunderstanding." The Magaddino Mafia began to distance itself from the Toronto mobsters. While Magaddino trusted Papalia, he apparently believed that Agueci would break Omerta; furthermore, word from Toronto told Magaddino that Alberto was restless, pacing, and to him, this meant Agueci was ready to break. Magaddino did not send bail or any help at all. Then, when Alberto's lawyer, a member of the Buffalo family, fumbled his case, Alberto blamed boss Don Stefano. He openly threatened Magaddino.

Bail was posted by Alberto's wife, who had to mortgage their house to do so. Alberto was furious. Since he and his compatriots had paid tribute money to Magaddino all along, he felt he deserved better. Whether it was purely distrust on Magaddino's part or greed that made him not honor his promise to Agueci, if a promise had been made, we can only guess. What we do know is that Alberto Agueci left Toronto for a meeting with Don Stefano after his bail. He was never seen alive again. One month later, in November 1961, hunters found his decomposing remains in a cornfield outside the small Rochester suburb of Penfield. It was an obvious mob hit. His hands were bound behind him with barbed wire; his fingerprints and face had been burned away. Naked and broken, he had been left as carrion, and the animals had feasted.

Fred "the Wolf" Randaccio had been with Magaddino for decades and had worked his way up in the ranks. It is believed that by the 1950s, Magaddino had given him most of the control, and he was poised to take over operations. It is also conjectured that he took part in plotting the 1963 assassination of President John F. Kennedy, though hard evidence could not be found.

Things began to fall apart with a raid on a bachelor party for alleged boss Joseph Todaro in Buffalo in May 1967 and his arrest a month later on charges of conspiracy to commit bank robbery. Randaccio was one of many convicted and sent "up the river" to do serious time. This left his powerful position with the Arm open and available. His second in command, Sam Pieri, wanted the job, but Magaddino named his own son, Peter, instead. A rift formed in the once cohesive and powerful Magaddino family.

Magaddino's reign was coming to an end. He held the last of the three traditional seats on the commission, and at age seventy-seven in 1968, he and his son Peter were arrested on charges of interstate bookmaking, along with others in the family. When police raided his son's house, they found a suitcase containing almost $500,000. All charges were dropped because authorities did not want to name their informant, and any wiretaps they had used had been illegal. But the damage to Magaddino was far worse than jail time; he lost face with his family. He was losing his old supporters and could no longer control the actions of his associates.

In 1974, Don Stefano passed after a heart attack and faded into history. His legacy? Well, the stories say that his funeral at St. Joseph's Church in Niagara Falls was well attended and that the police stood outside and wrote down the license plate numbers of the many people who came to pay their respects.

One last note on Don Stefano Magaddino: he was not just nicknamed the Undertaker because of his crime business. His "legitimate" business was a funeral home in Niagara Falls, New York. Stories abound about how this front business might have been used. While it is known that legitimate funerals were held at the location, Magaddino is rumored to have been a greedy man, and some say false bottoms on many coffins leaving the home for burial hid additional bodies. Whether or not they were men Magaddino's gang killed, the stories are deliciously wicked.

The Magaddino Memorial Chapel at 1338 Niagara Street was recently named as part of a project called the "Niagara Falls Gateway Redevelopment Project" to be redesigned and reconfigured for use as administration offices of some kind. This is under dispute as some feel there might be better use for the proposed $400,000.

Magaddino's other Niagara Falls businesses included the Power City Distributing Company and the Camellia Linen Supply Company and possibly an exterminating company. It certainly does make one pause to wonder what was being distributed, laundered and exterminated!

Perhaps most chilling are stories that when the House Assassinations Committee met to look at the deaths of John F. Kennedy, Robert Kennedy and Martin Luther King in 1979, Stefano Magaddino was heard on tape talking about the need to kill JFK and his family. Because words are not actions and no evidence was found to connect the Mafia with the events, Stefano Magaddino was never charged, and the Mafia was considered not to be involved. However, the FBI did not discount the fact that some members may have acted alone, and many conspiracy theorists still believe the Mafia played a role in the assassinations.

Anatomy of a Fallen Empire

After Don Stefano's death, Papalia supposedly ran the Ontario business until he was murdered in 1997. The struggle for control over Magaddino's empire in the United States began even before he passed.

Russell Bufalino, Sicilian born, began his life of crime as a teenager in Buffalo, New York, after immigrating here with his family in the early 1900s. His mentors were some of the region's future Mafia big bosses. Bufalino's first boss was John C. Montana, labor racketeer and a very important figure in Magaddino's organization. Montana also owned one of Western New York's largest taxi companies, held a seat on the Buffalo City Council and was voted "Man of the Year" in 1956. Montana was exposed after Apalachin.

Bufalino had a record of multiple arrests by the time he was in his twenties and became associated with Joseph Barbara, the man whose ranch was later used for the Apalachin Summit. Bufalino left Buffalo for Endicott, New York, the territory of his new friend. When Barbara became northern Pennsylvania's boss, Bufalino was named underboss. Following Joseph Barbara's death in 1959, Bufalino took over as boss. In 1974, with the death of Don Stefano Magaddino, Bufalino began a more aggressive expansion of his family's business. He allegedly sent family members to the Niagara Region to set up both illegal business in gambling and also his "legitimate" business in real estate.

Magaddino's family was split, with leadership being taken by several members, and their supporters going with them. Following a 1968 meeting at the farmhouse of Frank Valenti, who headed up the business in Rochester, the Arm split into four factions: Magaddino, Salvatore Pieri and his right-hand man Frangiamore, Joseph Fino and Valenti, who took Rochester and left the Buffalo family. The commission no longer recognized Magaddino as head of the Buffalo family.

Salvatore Pieri had a brief but rather fruitless turn as boss from 1969 to 1970, followed by Joseph Fino, who was forced out by rivals in 1972. Another player was Sam "the Farmer" Frangiamore, who was recognized as boss from 1972 to 1974, when Magaddino died. At that time, the commission sanctioned Frangiamore as the head of the Buffalo family until the family could hold an election. It is believed that Frangiamore chose Pieri as his underboss. Some people argue that Pieri was boss until he died in 1981, after which Frangiamore held the role until 1984. Salvatore Pieri's brother Joe replaced him as underboss.

In May 1974, John Cammilleri, a reported corrupt labor official, was crossing a Buffalo street on his way to the funeral of another local mobster when he was gunned down. His murder began a string of mob-related killings that lasted until the mid-1980s. Cammilleri had been a longtime ranking member of the Arm. In 1939, Cammilleri returned to Buffalo after serving twenty years in Elmira Prison. He took a position with the Local 210 of the International Hod Carrier.

The 210 had a reputation as being a cover for many Buffalo Mafia members. In 1970, Cammilleri went head to head with Ron Fino, a business manager for the 210, and his father, Joseph Fino, who was trying to separate the mob from the union. As it turned out, Ron Fino was an undercover agent at the time and turned state's witness. During his testimony, he stated that his father had been another target, along with Cammilleri. Ron Fino went underground for protection, along with other witnesses.

Local 210, Buffalo, New York, an alleged haven for the mob. Hod carriers at Greenbelt, Maryland. *Courtesy of the Library of Congress Print and Photographs Division.*

A 1971 *U.S. Times* article tells the story of absolute corruption within Local 210 that slowed the construction of many Buffalo buildings. It states, "The Laborers' Union is a 'family' enterprise of the Stefano Magaddino Mob," and it names specific members.

The Cammilleri murder has never been solved.

You could almost hear the stones of the great empire Magaddino had worked so hard to build as they hit the ground. When he died, nothing was left that he would have recognized as his, except perhaps his funeral home.

Allegedly, Joseph Todaro Sr., a prominent Buffalo businessman, also known far and wide as "Lead Pipe Joe," took over as boss from Frangiamore. Todaro's son and brother were also said to be in the "family." Joseph Sr. was present at a 1968 meeting when it was decided that the Buffalo family should distance itself from Magaddino. Bosses across the country favored Todaro for the Buffalo seat. Old and young believed he could reunite the family and breathe new life into it. He achieved the position of boss because he was well liked.

Why didn't underboss Joe Pieri get elected instead of Todaro? He might have if Todaro had not spent years setting himself up to be liked by so many other bosses. It was a clever move. The commission recognized Todaro. Pieri was not happy, but Todaro set things right. He named his son, Joseph "Big Joe" Todaro Jr., as his underboss and Joe Pieri as his consigliore.

Todaro had things up and running and in good order with strengthened ties in Canada by 1985. Buffalo became a hub for bookmaking while maintaining its business in loan sharking, gambling and racketeering, much of it allegedly through the Local 210. The family later expanded its territory to Las Vegas and southern Florida.

Both Joseph Todaro Sr. and Joseph Jr. were named along with loan shark Leonard Falzone; Frank "Butchie Bifocals" BiFulco, the pension fund administrator; Joe Pieri and his brother, John; and twenty-six others in a complaint against Arthur Coia, acting president of the Local 210 Union. Hearings took place as recently as 1996 within the union under the watchful eye of the Department of Federal Justice. The accused called Ron Fino and other witnesses "hired liars."

The Local 210 has been trying to rebuild its good reputation ever since. In 1999, U.S. District Judge Richard Arcara scheduled a hearing to suggest that a court liaison be appointed to oversee operations of the 210. In 2010, the union tipped off New York State to violations of wage laws.

Today, the Todaros have a strong, legitimate business in Buffalo. They started and still own a popular area pizzeria, which has given donations to charity and to the military, including a generous feast of pizza and wings upon the visit of President Clinton in 1998.

Joseph Todaro Jr. is a highly respected businessman in Buffalo, and any criminal involvement is alleged. None of the Todaro family has ever been convicted of a crime.

Is the Mafia still in business in Buffalo and Niagara Falls? Some say yes, but nobody is talking. Who is at the helm? The truth has entered the realm of legend, and everyone claims Omerta.

Ghosts of the Past

Asylum

She was insane, a lunatic, crazy, a danger to herself and society. She was someone's mother, someone's daughter, someone's wife and someone's sister. He was insane, too. There was only one thing to do with such people. We told ourselves it was for their own good. We believed we could not help them. They were institutionalized, and they were the lucky ones, perhaps.

The asylums of the eighteenth century were hellish places. Among them was the St. Mary Bethlehem Hospital in London, more commonly known as Bedlam. In that asylum, they charged a penny admission for the public to come and watch the "show." This raised money for the hospital.

One of the earliest songs written about the insane is a chilling and eerie reminder of those past days. "Bedlam Boys" was introduced in 1618:

For to see Mad Tom of Bedlam,
Ten thousand miles I've travelled.
Mad Maudlin goes on dirty toes,
For to save her shoes from gravel.

Still I sing bonney boys, Bonney mad boys,
Bedlam boys are bonney,
For they all go bare, and they live by the air,
And they want no drink nor money.

I went down to Satan's Kitchen
For to get me food one morning
And there I got souls piping hot
All on the spit a-turning.

There were no formal institutions in America in which to place mentally unstable individuals until concerned citizens such as Boston's Dorothea Dix became major advocates for more humane treatment of the mentally ill. With their staunch efforts, hospitals for the insane were established in America. Central to the work of these crusaders was the philosophy of individualized care without economic discrimination; poor and wealthy were placed together to ensure equal-quality care. By the time America built its first asylums, Europe had already begun to develop new theories for treatment, the most highly recommended being "moral treatment."

The mid-nineteenth to mid-twentieth centuries might be called the age of the asylum in America. There were hundreds, perhaps thousands, across the country, and each was packed to overflowing in many instances, though they didn't begin that way. New York State had several "lunatic" asylums, and the Niagara Region had one of the most famous (or infamous): the Buffalo State Asylum for the Insane.

Patients in these institutions were fortunate, if only because their predecessors throughout history had been cast away and forgotten in dungeons, prisons or poorhouses; were forced to beg on the streets; had holes drilled in their heads; and were accused of witchcraft, tortured or even burned at the stake. It was believed that they were possessed by demons.

Right up until the early nineteenth century, difficult patients were placed in coffin-like boxes with sliding doors across the small openings, where their faces could be seen; seated in chairs with paddles securing their heads and straps across their arms; or wrapped in straight jackets or with chained belts about the waist. Drugged, submerged in ice-cold water, shocked and hung in swings, they were completely at the mercy of their caregivers—if care even belongs in that phrase.

The mid- to late nineteenth-century ushered in the "kinder, gentler" age of the moral treatment system, which was first developed in Europe by Quaker William Tuke. This system suggested that a pleasant environment, removal from families and relationships that were unstable, occupational

Darwin-Coxe machine, in which the insane were swung until quiet. "Fool Tower," Vienna. *Courtesy of the Library of Congress Print and Photographs Division.*

English coffin for confining the insane. "Fool Tower," Vienna. *Courtesy of the Library of Congress Print and Photographs Division.*

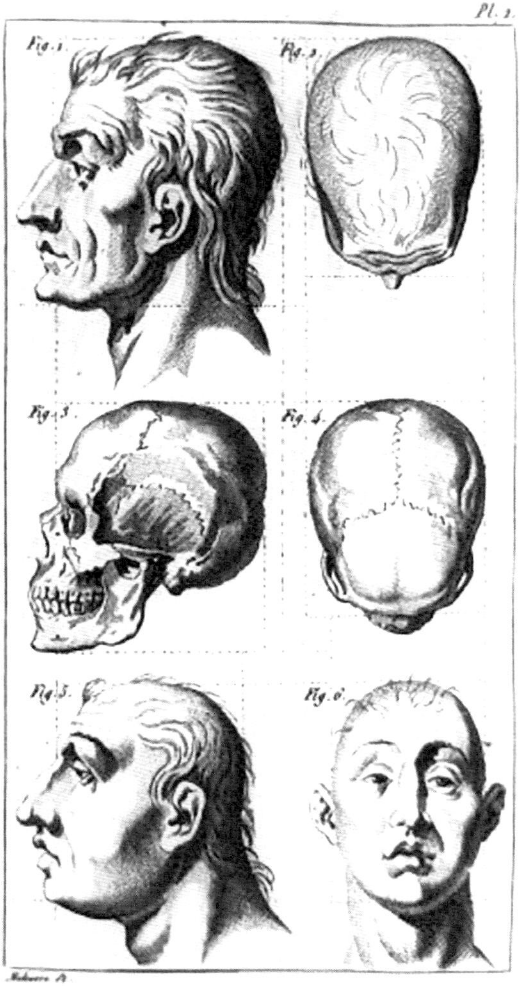

Cranial shape of the skull of a sane man in Figures 3 and 4 compared to the skull shape of an insane man. *Courtesy of the Library of Congress Print and Photographs Division.*

therapy, peace and quiet and less intrusive restraint of difficult "inmates" was far superior to the old medieval methods of curing the spirit with violence. Challenging old ideas that demons caused insanity, the moral system emphasized the environment as a cure for cases of mental illness as long as they were not chronic cases. New evidence pointed to brain damage as a cause of insanity. But unfortunately, even the best-laid plans cannot always foresee the restrictions under which they must function, and many of these new hospitals fell to corruption of one kind or another.

The philosophy of moral treatment suffered following the end of the American Civil War. Many professionals who once felt it was useful fell back on their old ways of thinking, adding to their ideas that insanity was hereditary and affected by upbringing and that personal behavior could be responsible for one's mental condition. At this time, doctors reverted to the use of drugs to keep patients under control. By the 1880s, the institutions for the insane had lost much favor with the public. Commissions were formed to investigate and oversee their operations. They were no longer called asylums but hospitals. The experiment of the moral system had failed to meet expectations. But by the end of this period, neurologists had developed new ideas—many of them sound, but others dubious, such as electric shock and the "rest cure." The rest cure was often used for hysteria in women. They were imprisoned for up to two years with little outside contact.

It was also during this period, from 1871 to 1890, that the Buffalo State Asylum for the Insane was planned, built and utilized. The full complex was not completed until 1895 and did not close its doors until 1974.

Bridging Medicine and the Environment

Among the supporters of moral therapy was Dr. Thomas Story Kirkbridge. Only half of his patients returned to function normally in society; nevertheless, his contribution was significant at a time when little was being done for these people. After years of studying medicine and spending time with the mentally ill, Kirkbridge developed theories on architectural design for asylums and wrote a volume titled *On the Construction, Organization, and General Arrangements of Hospitals For the Insane*. Many states, recreating their treatment systems under pressure from advocacy groups, utilized this plan, and New York was one of those states.

The Kirkbridge Plan was both an architectural design and a philosophy; in fact, it was a movement. Building on the ideologies of the moral system of compassion and equal treatment for insane persons, Kirkbridge devised a plan that included the occupational therapies he had witnessed when visiting Worcester State Hospital in Massachusetts. There, he had seen patients not only receiving medical treatment but also working in gardens, taking rides and going on walks.

Kirkbridge's building design was "V" shaped, often described as a flight of geese. It included a central administrative building with wings for patient wards—men on one side, women on the other. The administrative building also housed the superintendent and his family, and directly behind it were accessory buildings—a kitchen, auditorium, library and chapel. The wards were designed in such a way that patients could be housed according to their needs and by category of their severity. This configuration gave a Kirkbridge building something older asylums

State Hospital, Buffalo, New York. *Courtesy of the author.*

did not have: plenty of light, ventilation and a view of the manicured grounds. The Kirkbridge Plan was the plan used for the Buffalo State Asylum for the Insane.

BUFFALO STATE ASYLUM FOR THE INSANE

While Kirkbridge planned the configuration of buildings, Henry Hobson Richardson, who was on the cusp of his fame at that time, created the interior and exterior designs of Buffalo State Asylum (BSA). He is regarded as one of the three top American architects, the others being Louis Sullivan and Frank Lloyd Wright. Buffalo has buildings by all three.

Planners assembled a team for creating the full effect for BSA, including Richardson for the architecture and renowned landscaper Frederick Law Olmsted, who was responsible for most of Buffalo's parks and open spaces. Together, they produced a unique two-hundred-acre complex with the Kirkbridge plan at its center.

The building style is known as Richardsonian Romanesque, as Richardson is accredited with the style's revival. For his administrative building, the architect designed a pair of medieval towers, each 185 feet tall. Though they were and continue to be purely decorative, they pierce the sky at 400 Forest Avenue and are impossible to resist visually. They seem to announce a solid foundation, an undeniable power and strength, and suggest stability. Yet they are strangely haunting and severe in their appearances. One almost expects to see Dr. Frankenstein on the rooftop probing the sky for electricity, while bolts of lightning flash back and forth between the towers.

In addition to the main building, ten pavilions branched off from each end, five to the east and five to the west. It was Richardson's largest project at 400,000 square feet, but sadly he died before its completion.

Olmsted and his partner, Calvert Vaux, produced a landscape reminiscent of a chateau that was both ornamental and functional. Included were large open spaces around the buildings for quiet recreation. The designers worked hard to maintain the integrity of the treatment philosophies to be practiced in this facility. They utilized winding walkways and shade trees for calming patients. The land behind the buildings was a one-hundred-acre farm where the asylum grew most of its own food. Patients worked the farm as part of their therapeutic prescriptions. Today, this farmland is occupied for the most part by Buffalo State College.

Patients were to be treated with respect, but there were instances where long-sleeved jackets and sheet wraps were needed to protect them from self-injury. Also, the moral treatment meant having a chapel for worship and a library. Supposedly, the BSA had over seven hundred books available, as well as entertainments, dances and outings for patients who were able to function socially. In keeping with the ideology that occupational therapy was part of the cure for insanity and that idle hands were the devil's playground, patients worked in the institution's shops, which included a bakery, laundry, kitchen and sewing room, among others. This was truly a small city within walls. Women performed light housekeeping chores, such as changing bedding and dusting, and men helped tend the grounds and manage the farm.

All intentions of the BSA were to be above standard for the best care of its proposed six hundred patients. This hospital was state of the art and one of the most progressive of its time. There were sitting rooms with fireplaces and dining rooms; the halls were brightly illuminated and were large enough for indoor recreation. But for all of this, the institution was unable to maintain its ideals, and what began as a great experiment in humanity ended in brutality and shameful mismanagement.

THE NIGHT SHIFT

One cannot blame the planners, or really the physicians, who developed the building, treatments and individualized care for patients at Buffalo State Asylum. They could not have known at the time that their ideas would be challenged; nor could they have known that the demands placed on the facility would grow so rapidly.

The first major influence that put strain on the mental health system came with the end of the Civil War in 1865. Shell shock and other trauma suffered by soldiers during the war created a high demand for hospitalization in the country's institutions. While the BSA had not yet broken ground, when it did open in 1880, it was only partially complete, and already there were patients from other overcrowded institutions ready to fill its beds. Following World War I and World War II, another influx of war patients overwhelmed the already stressed facilities. Originally designed for six hundred inpatients, by 1940, the number of patients at the BSA had quadrupled to twenty-six hundred.

At the same time war-related psychiatric patients were competing for beds already taken by nonmilitary patients, doctors and nurses had to learn new systems for treatment. From 1910 through the 1960s, a new theory supplanted the system of moral treatment. The mental hygienic movement emphasized early intervention, prevention and promotion of mental health, but new ways of thinking take time to become ingrained and money to implement. Of course, Sigmund Freud was becoming an influence as well. The result of this shift was the addition of children into the mental health system. The BSA added an adolescent wing in 1969, when it demolished three buildings on the east wing to do so.

The population of the hospital was already beyond its capacity, and during World War II, when rationing hit the nation, the facility found itself running out of food. Though it had grown much of what it needed on its farmland, there were just too many people to feed with what it could produce. It was just more than the once self-sustaining facility could bear. It is interesting to note that the asylum originally made all of its own bedsheets in facility sewing rooms, as well as its own electricity. One report says that it used ten barrels of flour per day and over eight thousand tons of coal annually.

Then, to make matters worse, state and federal governments could not afford financial support or food for most of the prisons and hospitals nationwide.

With medical personnel making a mere $1,200 to $1,700 in annual wages, the number of qualified doctors, nurses and attendants dropped disproportionately per patient. One attendant might have as many as 150 patients to tend. This turned off the metaphorical light of the new age of mental health and forced the BSA and many other mental hospitals back into the dark ages.

War-era newspaper articles claimed that the hospital could not find enough food to feed its patients. BSA superintendent Dr. Fletcher stated, "We have no cheese on hand. We are unable to buy dried fruits, cocoa, dates and tapioca. We have no veal." He went on to talk about rationing butter and buying some eggs at local markets. A 1944 article from the *Buffalo Courier Express* further supported the overcrowding and poor staff wage situations. This article talked about the horrible conditions in the hospital.

Patients who were supposed to be given home-like, loving and gentle individualized attention were now in rows of beds lining the corridors that were once intended for recreation and to give insane patients a sense of space. Almost half of the patients at that time were elderly and mostly sat in their wards and did nothing. The goal for these patients became an effort to simply make their remaining years comfortable. Younger patients were still required to take occupational therapy, such as working in the facility's laundry and gardens, but with inadequate staff to watch over them, these activities were not as prevalent as intended by those who conceived the original plan. Workers demanded more pay and supervisors tried to get it, but you can't bleed money from a stone. There was just no increase to be had.

A direct result of overcrowding, rationing and poorly compensated staff was brutality, which was slow to be reported and dealt with. Until it was, patients were beaten, pummeled, kicked, unduly restrained and verbally abused, and some of their basic needs were ignored so more difficult patients could be tended. Many times patients were tied with towels or wrapped in sheets or thrown into confinement. But the BSA was not alone.

Life magazine published an article by reporter Albert Q. Maisel on May 6, 1946. It was titled "Bedlam 1946: Most U.S. Mental Hospitals are a Shame and a Disgrace." His knowledge was based on court reports, newspaper articles and his own observations, aided by reports from conscientious objectors who had taken service as attendants in the hospitals in lieu of the war. In the article, he talks about firetraps and patients sleeping on bare floors and running around without clothing. He reports their unkempt appearances, unnecessary restraints and living in "filth and feces." He further states that tuberculosis was thirteen times more common in the institutions. He also noted beatings, broken windows even in cold weather and menus that promised nourishment to make state inspectors happy when actually the patients were living on starvation diets.

Still I sing bonney boys, Bonney mad boys,
Bedlam boys are bonney,
For they all go bare, and they live by the air,
And they want no drink nor money.

It wasn't until the 1950s that inadequately tested drugs, electroshock, insulin shock (which did put the patient in a coma), fever therapy and lobotomies were mostly replaced with antipsychotic drugs. Still, these new treatments could not overcome the lack of qualified staff for patients.

Rumors throughout the 1960s and 1970s eluded to mistreatment, embezzlement, starvation, suicides and unexplained deaths. Finally, as a result of lawsuits and court rulings, state and federal laws were enacted leading to the salvation of mentally ill individuals. These new laws enabled individuals to refuse treatment and choose not to be institutionalized unless they posed a clear and present danger to themselves or others. New York State was forced to comply and to improve the conditions of its hospitals. This ultimately resulted in the state's decision to close many of its facilities, including Buffalo State Hospital, as it was known by 1974.

The Richardson Complex remains abandoned to this day but is renowned internationally as a great architectural treasure. It is listed on both the State and National Registers of Historic Places and as a National Historic Landmark. Some of its interior was used in the movie *The Natural*. Treatment for outpatients continued at the complex until the late 1990s. The main buildings are crumbling and deteriorating, while current restoration groups are attempting to find funding for refurbishing the site.

One must ask if the complex is haunted. If you believe that spirits might be tied to places where they died or suffered, or where they might have unfinished business, then it is quite possible that the Richardson Complex is haunted. The deplorable conditions under which these poor souls were kept after being entrusted to the care of the state are enough to make anyone

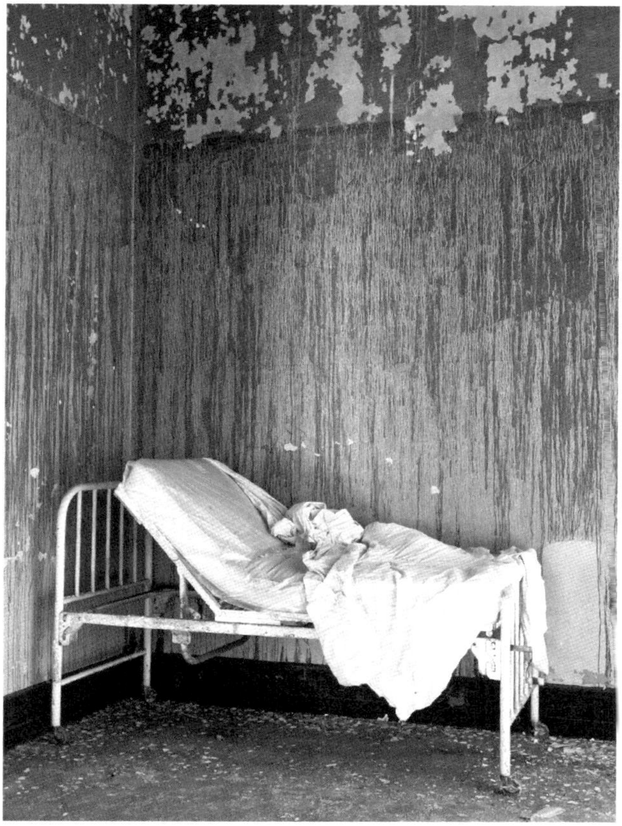

Abandoned bed from the Buffalo Asylum. "It was as if someone snapped their fingers and they all disappeared." *Courtesy of photographer Shaun O'Boyle.*

have nightmares. Perhaps there were doctors and nurses who wished they could have done more for their charges. It is reasonable that they might still be trying to do so. Amateur photographers have taken videos that have shown strange anomalies. Even though the facility is dangerous and off limits to the public, young people have taken dares. One trespasser said, "It was as if someone snapped their fingers and they all disappeared." And it's true—everyone, both patients and staff, did "vanish," leaving beds and furnishings and some equipment just as it was. They are all gone now, but with this story they cannot disappear from our memories. We will continue to whisper their tales.

The spirits white as lightning
Will on my travels guide me

The stars would shake and the moon would quake
Whenever they espied me.

Still I sing bonney boys, Bonney mad boys,
Bedlam boys are bonney,
For they all go bare, and they live by the air,
And they want no drink nor money.

And when that I'll be murdering
The man in the moon to a powder
His staff I'll break and his dog I'll shake
And there'll howl no demon louder.

DEVIL'S HOLE

Native peoples, French explorers, the British, Americans, trolleys and tourists have come and gone in and around the bowl-shaped cleft in the wall of the Niagara gorge known as Devil's Hole. Deep, steep, treacherous and alluring, it stirs the imagination. The once heavily treed landscape above the gorge was used for centuries as a portage trail to circumvent Niagara Falls, and later, the area above and below the rim became popular with tourists for enjoyment of its natural beauty.

Located four miles from Niagara Falls, Devil's Hole was slowly worn into the rock by what became known as Bloody Run, one of ancient Lake Tonawanda's many distributaries, which included Niagara Falls. Twelve thousand years ago, the two runoffs met at the Devil's Hole site, emptying into the Niagara River, now three hundred feet below. Eventually, with population growth and development, Bloody Run became what it is today—no more than a trickle after a rain. Lake Tonawanda, created by receding glaciers, disappeared thousands of years ago, but it left a footprint in the form of geological formations and their stories.

Approximately seventy feet below the park level is a cave thirty feet deep, carved by years of turbulent waters. Once much more extensive, the cave was known to the ancient peoples as the Cave of the Evil Spirit. The Great Serpent issued forth from this cave to devour whatever lay in its path. This was the Great Horned Serpent that made the people sick, so they tried to appease it with sacrifices. This cave, the natives warned, would bring ill fortune to any who entered.

French explorer Robert de La Salle was told of its power, but he didn't believe. Out of curiosity or perhaps the pull of the cave itself, he entered in 1679, and later, in 1687, he was shot by one of his own mutineering men, stripped of his clothes and valuables and left to die somewhere in what is now Texas. Some stories say La Salle heard voices in the cave that gave him prophecies in the language of the Iroquois. The voices promised greatness to be followed by his sudden death, all of which came true. His fate was violent and has become part of the Devil's Hole legend.

The French and Indian War had barely ended. In 1761, the British, who held Fort Niagara since their capture of it in 1759, ruled the once French stronghold of the Niagara Peninsula. Now, the British controlled the portage trail that the Indians had considered theirs for centuries before the white man came.

Though not in great number, British colonists were coming, slowing trickling in from the east and homesteading these once native lands. The French had been benevolent fathers to the Indians, though the natives preferred to think of it as a symbiotic relationship, meaning that they still had rights, freedoms and control over their lives. Sir William Johnson, British general, Indian agent and adopted brother to the Iroquois, considered the Indians as equals, but his superiors took a more distant stance, considering the natives potential threats to be subjugated. The soldiers in their forts and the civilians settling on the land gave little thought to those who had been there before them. In the eyes of the Indians, they were locusts devouring their way of life.

The Indians who lived in the region had controlled the portage for as long as they could remember, and the French had utilized them, paying them for their services as guides and porters. But the British knew how vital that portage was to their survival as rulers of this land and to the supplies they had to transport from their Atlantic colonies to their westernmost outposts. A small fort named Fort Schlosser guarded the upper terminus of the portage that ran from Fort Niagara at the mouth of the river at Lake Ontario up the escarpment to Lake Erie via the Niagara River. Boats transported supplies from Schlosser to destinations on the upper Great Lakes.

When the British took control of the portage trail, General Sir William Johnson placed John Stedman in charge, and as the new portage master he set about to improve the trail's condition. The footpath was widened to accommodate supply wagons and to eliminate the need for Indian porters.

As is sometimes the case, events come together with such timing that we might find it difficult to determine which influenced which. The improvements basically left the Indians without the paid labor they once had under the French and took away their control. This coincided with a rebellion brewing under the leadership of an Ottawa chief, Pontiac, who despised his people's dependency on the white man and believed it would be best to drive all white men from the land. He persuaded many other chiefs and their followers to join his war. In May 1763, the boiling kettle overflowed into attacks on many forts and settlements. Hundreds of settlers were killed or captured. It was within this political climate that one of the Niagara Region's most horrific events took place: the Devil's Hole Massacre.

A SUNNY, BLOOD-SOAKED DAY, SEPTEMBER 14, 1763

Early to mid-September in the Niagara Region is usually pleasant. If we have an early Indian summer, it can be downright hot, but this September day was fair and sunny.

William Matthews fastened the last button on his uniform, placed the hat on his head and picked up his drum. It was time to summon the men to form up for a routine return to Fort Niagara. The wagons loaded with supplies from boats on Lake Ontario had traveled from Fort Niagara along the portage trail through Lewiston to Fort Schlosser and had been unloaded and made ready for the journey home. William went through the various beats in his head and then tapped them out on the drum's rim. These were signals that could be heard over whatever other noises there might be—the roar of the falls, the din of battle or a man who just hoped for one more hour of sleep. He knew them well; it was his job, and it could be that with a drum signal he might even save someone's life. The drummer boy straightened his back proudly at that thought and carried out his duty.

That was how the day began for young William Matthews and twenty-three others. Teams were hitched to the empty wagons, and the company of soldiers, a few teamsters and civilians set off on the portage trail toward Fort

Niagara. They were aware of the dangers along the paths and the fact that the Indians were on edge, but overall it was a routine mission. The drummer beat a slow walk and allowed his mind to wander with the beat; it was second nature to him. The leaves had begun to fall, but there were still many on the trees now turning fully into the golds, oranges and reds that made this country so beautiful. Treacherous though the trail might be, to William it was a most wonderful place.

They walked throughout the morning, and upon reaching Devil's Hole, a wooded area with difficult terrain, their leader, master of the portage John Stedman, halted them. William's drum fell silent; in fact, they all hushed, and William could feel the blood rushing through his heart it was beating so fast. The leader took one more step forward with a kind of nod, as if to say he was mistaken, when all hell broke loose.

The trail was suddenly alive with musket fire from the trees. Flights of arrows and whooping Indians seemed to leap from out of thin air. They had been waiting in ambush among trees and rocks, quietly blending in with their surroundings, until they had the wagon train hemmed in against the precipice. The supply party could not have known the odds were stacked against them as they were besieged with the sudden round of fire. At such close quarters, a return volley was impossible, and the party was set upon by at least three hundred Indians against its twenty-four. They were no match for the tomahawks and clubs that descended upon them.

The silent wood was now a mass of blood, broken bodies, screaming men and savage cries of victory from the Indians. The wagon teams broke loose or ran with wagons still hitched, some to the edge of the precipice and over. Horses, oxen, wagons and men fell, were pushed or were thrown to the rocks below. Some, rather than face scalping or torture, preferred their chances with the fall and dove over the edge, including drummer boy William Matthews.

His hat flew off his head, the drum went flying from his hands and down, down, down the boy fell, the air around him filled with the dead and those who soon would be—all a blur to him. It is said that the stream ran red that day and was ever after called Bloody Run, though there are other stories of how it got its name.

John Stedman escaped the carnage on horseback to make his way back to Fort Schlosser for reinforcements. The gunfire was heard in the distance at

Fort Grey in Lewiston, one of several stockades that ranged between Forts Niagara and Schlosser. Stationed there, the British Eightieth Regiment raced to the wagon train's aid. They, too, were cut down only a mile or so from the first attack, with only eight men barely escaping; the rest were slaughtered and scalped. Stedman's reinforcements finally arrived, but by the time they did, it was over. The dead lay everywhere. Fearful of another attack, they returned to the fort. It was only after four days that they were able to collect the dead and their belongings. To their horror, most of the bodies had been scalped and mutilated and then tossed without ceremony into the gorge with wagons and other equipment that had not been pushed off during the battle.

They retrieved what they could from the piles of shattered wagons and broken, mutilated men, oxen and horses. Hats, rifles, packs and belongings were strewn from top to bottom; a drum, or what remained of it, was found where it had been thrown, and there were bodies in the trees like strange ornaments dangling for a macabre celebration. One of those bodies was that of a boy lodged in the branches of an old-growth tree, one with oak leaves turning the color of his uniform so that he had almost been missed. But he was alive.

Drummer boy William Matthews was one of only two or three survivors, depending on which account you read. He lived to be ninety years old and died in Queenston, Ontario. Another of the survivors was John Stedman, master of the portage, who lived in a house on the grounds of Fort Schlosser, the house that was once attached to the lonely stone chimney hidden among the trees along the Robert L. Moses Parkway. It still reaches to the sky and has many stories of its own to tell.

You will find Stedman's name connected with a few stories here. After the Devil's Hole Massacre, it was determined that Seneca Chief Farmer's Brother had organized that attack, and Sir William Johnson forced the Indians to cede a mile-wide strip of land that ran along the Niagara River from Lake Ontario to Lake Erie. The tract included the portage trail and several small upriver islands. Some of this land was granted to Stedman for his service, including a small island he called "the Goat's Island." This is where Stedman put his goats to keep them safe from marauders. Sadly, his animals did not survive. They were frozen to death during the frigid winter of 1780.

Pontiac's Rebellion has been blamed for the deeds done that day, as were the British for refusing to honor old promises made by the French for the

Indians' control of the trails and payment for their labors. Some mention has been made that this was perhaps the first labor uprising in America. For certain, the Cave of the Evil Spirit had its fill that day, and perhaps when conditions are right and a deep silence permeates the air, the sound of cries and war whoops might be heard at Devil's Hole, echoing through the gorge.

The result of the savagery was not as Pontiac and Farmer's Brother had intended. While the region remained wilderness until after the Revolutionary War, instead of the British leaving, they became more watchful and reinforced in their resolve.

This story was created with information from several sources, some giving different numbers of men on the mission and different numbers of survivors. Some accounts say the detail was heading with loaded wagons from Fort Niagara to Fort Schlosser, while others say just the opposite. All sources seem to agree that John Stedman led the wagon train and survived, along with at least one other, perhaps a boy drummer or perhaps a teamster or both. The most important piece of this story, however, is the terrible event that did occur at this location.

Today, the site is part of a forty-two-acre New York State Park designed by Frederick Law Olmsted and Calvert Vaux in 1887, the same landscape duo that designed many parks in Buffalo and the grounds of the Buffalo State Asylum. One can climb down the unstable stone steps that lead into the ravine, take a lunch and enjoy the scenery, but it isn't for the faint of heart. The path is dangerous and not recommended for children or those who are not physically fit. One tourist report says, "Despite the intimidating name, and proximity to certain death, the park is harmless for those that play safe, and certainly should not be avoided."

It is also not for those who fear the ghosts of the past. Even people who have merely viewed the cave from a distance or walked into the gorge have encountered tragedy. In 1895, the Niagara Gorge Belt Line Railroad opened the Great Gorge Route to take travelers, mostly tourists, from Niagara Falls to Lewiston. The electric trolley passed by Devil's Hole, making the ravine a popular tourist attraction, and some believe it provided a feast for the Great Serpent as year after year it brought tragedy.

Just hours before his assassination in 1901, President McKinley viewed the cave from the trolley. On March 12, 1907, an avalanche of ice killed a conductor and eight passengers. The conductor had gone ahead of the

President McKinley was shot at the Pan-American Exposition in Buffalo, New York, 1901. *Courtesy of the Library of Congress Print and Photographs Division.*

trolley to clear ice from a switch. A huge sheet of ice loosened from a slope and crushed him to death. The rest of it, weighing tons, crushed the trolley. There was a derailment following a head-on crash of two cars in 1910, and in another year, a garbage chute explosion spilled sewage on passengers. In 1915, thirteen people were killed and sixty injured in another derailment. This incident was due to an overloaded trolley from a Sunday school picnic. Then, in 1917, a trolley car suddenly flew from the tracks carrying nearly fifty people to their deaths in the Niagara River, and the Great Serpent had yet another sacrifice. Yes, all could be explained as the consequences of nature or man's foolishness, but all are unmistakably connected in some way to the gorge near Devil's Hole and its cave.

As recently as 2009, a thirty-three-year-old man fell into the gorge while hiking and died later in the emergency room. There have been hundreds of additional accidental deaths or suicides, and even murders, associated with the site. Hardly a year goes by without an incident. Even nearby Niagara University, founded by the Vincentian religious order and located across the

Giant Rock, Great Gorge Route (Niagara Gorge Railroad), Niagara Falls. *Courtesy of the Library of Congress Print and Photographs Division.*

Robert Moses Parkway from the park, has been plagued by fires since it was built. Some people attribute those fires to the strange energies here. In 1864, a fire swept through Clet Hall, the first building erected on the campus. A student named Thomas Hopkins was killed in that fire and is said to continue to roam the halls of the Clet building today, knocking on doors so others will not perish the way he did.

This once "sacred" place revered by the native peoples and feared by the early Jesuits is now marred by graffiti and trash. Local college students use the cave for parties. And there is that feeling that something is there, either the cave or the dead, waiting and watching as you carefully take your next step. It may just be imagination entwining itself with history and legend as so often happens.

Deeds Most Foul

Artistic Fungi

An artist can benefit greatly from a patron, and just prior to the turn of the 1900s, American industrialist Andrew Corbin urged Parisian artist Jules Henri Marchand to come to America to design hardware. After finding this work to be unsatisfactory to his artistic sensibilities, Henri Marchand landed a position with the New York State Museum in Albany in 1909.

Born near Paris, France, Marchand had studied art under the tutorage of famed sculpture Auguste Rodin. When he traveled to America, he brought with him his wife, Clotilde, also an artist. By the time they settled in Albany, the Marchands had two sons old enough to work with their father. In all, they had five children who later accompanied their parents to the city of Buffalo. The two older boys, Paul and George, worked side by side with their father and would give Buffalo a legacy that still exists today.

Henri Marchand was at that time a leader in the science and art of display for museums. He and his two sons created dioramas with wax figures depicting fossils and the lifestyle of the Native Americans. These exhibits remained open in the Albany museum for viewing until 1976, but perhaps the most striking works produced by the trio were those commissioned by friends of Charles Peck, botanist and American fungi expert. In 1917, the Marchands created fifty-seven beautifully realistic wax sculptures of mushrooms. Sadly, this collection is no longer available for viewing.

Jules Henri Marchand was less than forty years old as his fame began to spread throughout the country, and it was not long before the artist and his sons were offered other commissions. Henri eventually formed the Marchand Diorama Corporation, with its works on display at Chicago's Field Museum of Natural History, the Smithsonian and the American Museum of Natural History, all of which came after the event that rocked the Niagara Region like no other scandal, and for years it remained one of the most horrific murders in Buffalo's history.

The Collection

Less than a quarter century after Buffalo was burned to the ground during the War of 1812, a group of young men formed the Young Men's Association (YMA) to organize cultural events, as well as involving itself with the public library, the sciences and the arts. The year was 1836, and it was an era of wonder when many took an interest in the natural sciences, anthropology and archaeology, and of course, the strange and macabre were present as well. People flocked to circus sideshows and exhibitions, where they paid pennies to view artifacts and paintings, such as the famed painting *Trial of Red Jacket*, currently housed at the historical society in Buffalo, New York.

As was the custom in many communities during this era, the local libraries found themselves recipients of all manner of objects of curiosity, from rocks and minerals to insects, paintings and historical artifacts. As such, the YMA had acquired a large collection, so it installed a cabinet at the library that became the seed for the Buffalo Society of Natural Sciences, known today as the Buffalo Museum of Science.

The YMA circulated a petition of sorts to see what interest there might be in forming a group focused on the natural sciences, which proved to draw a good deal of attention, including the signature of Millard Fillmore, thirteenth president of the United States and a Buffalo resident. The group's first meeting was held in 1861. It was not until after meeting at several different locations that, on January 19, 1929, the society opened the doors to its permanent home on Humboldt Parkway in Buffalo.

Now with a permanent home for its collection, the Society of Natural Sciences needed someone to help organize its displays, so it turned to someone with great knowledge about such things—Jules Henri Marchand. His family had already moved to Buffalo in 1925 and settled into a home on Riley Avenue. Now, Henri and his sons began the work of making the museum world-renowned during the 1930s and '40s, with its beautiful detailed works in wax, painted backgrounds for diorama displays and expertly created environs, a perfect blend of science and art.

THE ART OF DECEPTION

Jules Henri Marchand, commonly called Henri, can best be described as an artist, businessman and collector, but some of what he collected could not be displayed in wax at the museum. Henri was a philanderer, a collector of women. His work often took him to the Cattaraugus Indian Reservation

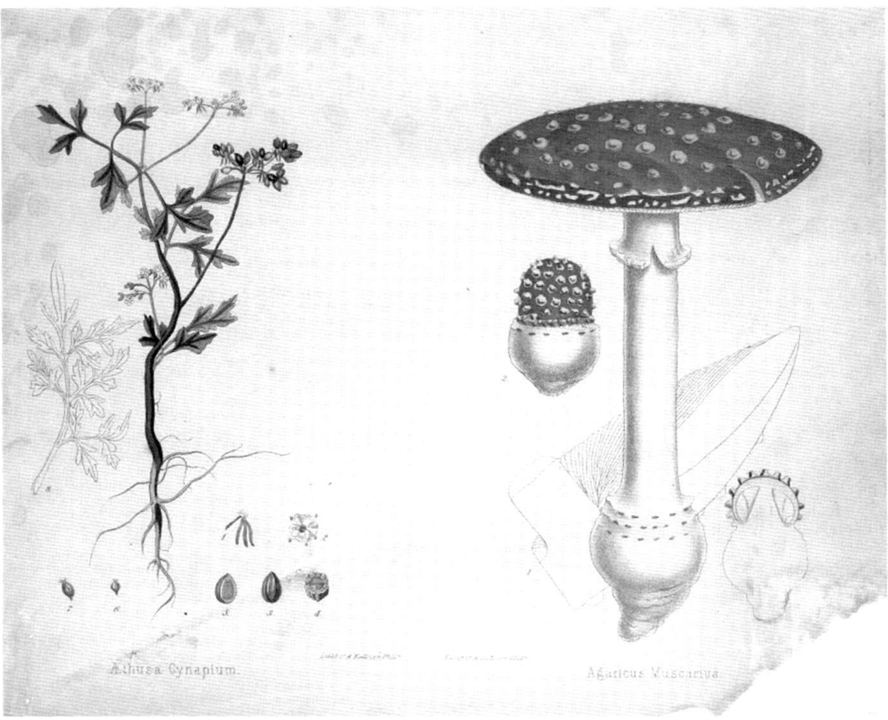

Mrs. Marchand gathered mushrooms. Print specimen of botanical illustrations for *Aethusa cynapium*. *Courtesy of the Library of Congress Print and Photographs Division.*

to study nature, and his wife, Clotilde, sometimes went with him to gather mushrooms and make her own sketches. But their time together in Buffalo was to be short, as Clotilde was murdered on March 6, 1930. It was a scandal filled with crime, prejudice and immorality that made the news worldwide.

During the trial following his wife's murder, Henri admitted that he slept around with many Indian women and claimed his wife knew it. According to Henri, she understood it was a "necessity of business." How else would he get the natives to show him their breasts so he could give his wax sculptures the most lifelike appearances? Indian women, it should be pointed out, were not the only women Henri slept with. There were others in New England and even in France. But it was not Henri who was on trial for the death of Clotilde Marchand. The murderer was one of two Indian women—"squaws," as the newspaper bluntly called them—one of whom Henri had spoken to of love, had pleasured and had sculpted. Henri admitted to being a "squaw man," and she was a thirty-five-year-old native from the Cattaraugus reservation, Lila Jimerson. The second women, also of the reservation and later convicted of the crime, was sixty-eight-year-old Nancy Bowen. Lila, according to testimony, had duped her into committing the foul deed.

Some versions of the story say that Henri Marchand owned a motorcar, and Lila Jimerson had told him she wanted a ride that March morning. Henri made some excuse to his wife or perhaps skipped from his work without her knowledge, leaving Clotilde alone at home and the children either working or at school. While he and his Indian mistress drove about town, a stranger came to the door of the Riley Avenue residence. It was the old Indian woman, whom the newspapers described as a bent and toothless Nancy Bowen. Testimony during the trial placed Lila Jimerson at a Buffalo hardware store waiting for her accomplice. Either way, the plot was dastardly.

Clotilde answered the door and invited the woman into her home. Speaking kindly to the stranger in a mix of broken English and French, Clotilde, a slight women, turned to lower the volume on the radio that sat on a cabinet next to the stairs. As soon as her back was turned, with a fury, Nancy Bowen leaped on Clotilde, grabbing her by the throat and stuffing a chloroform-soaked paper into her mouth. She then struck the unsuspecting woman twice on the head with a hammer purchased earlier that day. When Henri Jr., the Marchand's twelve-year-old son, arrived home from school that afternoon, he found his mother crumpled at the bottom of the stairs in a pool of blood. The boy ran for help at the museum, where his father and brothers would have been.

When the detectives arrived, they first deduced that Mrs. Marchand must have fallen down the stairs. Her position at the bottom of the stairs and the overturned radio cabinet made this logical. She had tripped and fallen, grabbing at the cabinet to steady herself without success. The cabinet was on top of her, and she must have hit her head against the stair post.

The coroner, after examining Clotilde and finding the chloroform-soaked paper in her mouth, felt the wounds were more reminiscent of murder than accidental death. While one wound was from hitting her head on the post, the other two were made with a blunt weapon. He reported that Mrs. Marchand had struggled for her life, as her knuckles and arms were bruised. There were finger marks about her neck indicating a slender hand. Police ruled out robbery, as nothing of value was taken from the home. Henri and a museum worker, who was boarding with the Marchands at the time, were taken in for questioning. Following that questioning, detectives were dispatched with orders to keep their destination secret.

The people of the Niagara Region had never experienced anything quite like this before, and of course, people were concerned that there might be a killer at large. While it turned out that neither Henri Marchand nor the boarder, Edward Burmeister, were considered suspects, another woman living in an upper flat of that house did say a strange man had come to her door two weeks prior asking about a man named Charles Ackerman, whom he believed lived at that address. Strangely, Ackerman had been reported missing for several weeks. As it turned out, the two cases were not related, but at that time, the police had to consider all the possibilities.

After questioning Henri and Edward, the police made a reasonable guess that the motive for the murder was jealousy. Neighbors told police that they had seen an Indian woman lurking about before the murder, and since Henri had worked on the reservation, the police asked him if perhaps the killer might be an Indian. Henri Marchand gave the police a description of his "model." It was discovered that the suspect had left the Marchand home and taken a bus from downtown Buffalo at 6:00 p.m. Detectives apprehended Lila Jimerson at the reservation, and she implicated Nancy Bowen as the one who had committed the crime. The police were not cautious in their dealings with the residents on the reservation; they tore through private homes searching for evidence. Some of Clotilde's personal effects were finally found in Bowen's possession, but the murder weapon was never found. In addition, a piece of eyeglass lens was found at the scene of the crime, and it matched the remnants of a pair of glasses discovered in Nancy's house. Yes, she had been at the Marchand home.

The two women were taken into custody. Lila Jimerson, whose Indian name meant "Lilac," was dubbed the "Red Lilac" by the press. She was the junior of Clotilde by almost eleven years and was thirteen years younger than Henri. Lila claimed to be madly in love with the French artist and said he returned the sentiment, not only in action and spoken words but also in letters. What came out at the trial can be called nothing if not strange and sensational.

Murdering the "White Witch"

No doubt, Lila had dark thoughts that set into motion the events of March 6, 1930. She possibly wondered how she could be so hopelessly enamored of Henri and continue to share him with that women, his wife. But how could she, an Indian woman, persuade him to leave his wife? It was impossible. What if Clotilde were to meet with an accident? But Lila couldn't do it herself; no, she would have to find someone else and give a good reason to kill Mrs. Marchand. Any of these thoughts might have run through Lila Jimerson's mind as she imagined a life with the well-known artist and luxuries she had never known before.

Nancy Bowen lost her husband, Chief Charley "Sassafras" Bowen. He was dead, and she wanted to know why. Lila decided that Nancy, whom some believed to be a medicine woman, might be just the one to rid her of Henri's wife. If only Lila could somehow blame the white woman for Charley's death. Lila had previously met Mrs. Marchand at the reservation and had seen her collecting mushrooms. She no doubt knew that the native people did not tolerate witchcraft. Lila Jimerson decided to accuse Mrs. Marchand of being a witch, and she went to Nancy to make that claim.

Ouija boards, an idea dating back to ancient China, were made popular as a divining tool by an American spiritualist during World War I. Some people believed the board could allow the living to communicate with the dead. Most people thought of the board as a parlor game, but Lila had a much different use in mind. Perhaps the dead could help Lila make her point with Nancy, and maybe Charley would tell them who was responsible for his death.

The two women sat with the Ouija board between them and placed their hands on the planchette, the piece used to spell out words on the board. The women called on Sassafras Charley, and the planchette glided slowly, with small jerking movements, across the face of the Ouija.

"Are you there?" the women asked.

"Yes," was the reply.

"How are you?" Nancy asked.

"I'm hungry."

"Well, is everything else alright?"

"They buried me like a rag doll."

Nancy and Lila continued to ask directing questions until they finally asked, "How did you die?"

"T-h-e-y…k-i-l-l-e-d…m-e."

When the women asked who "they" were, the board fell silent. The two women brought the board out on subsequent occasions, and then finally one night Nancy asked again, "Who did it Charley?" The board spelled out the name "Clotilde," and along with her address, it gave her description. The reason for his death, the old chief said, was "jealousy."

Following the séance, several handwritten letters were sent to Nancy Bowen, all signed by "Mrs. Dooley," a supposed spiritualist. The letters said that Mrs. Marchand was a witch who had put a spell on Nancy's man. One letter even went so far as to say the spell had failed, so Clotilde decided to kill Charley. Nancy believed Clotilde would come for her as well.

Prejudice abounded throughout the first trial. District attorney Guy Moore more than once referred to Lila Jimerson as a "filthy Indian." Jimerson went into that trial without government defense. Native American elders vehemently opposed not only the language that was used concerning the Indians but also the lack of legal support given to the defendant. Washington would not help because the Indians had signed their treaty with New York State. They were not under protection of the U.S. government as were many other tribes. The defense attorneys supplied were a reservation attorney and two from the court.

Eventually, the United States government did take an interest in the case with the Indians as wards, but not until Tuscarora chief Clinton Rickard sent a request to U.S. district attorney Richard H. Templeton. Chief

Rickard was the 1926 founder of the Indian Defense League of America, an organization started to protect further loss of Native American rights. He and many others cried foul. Of course, it didn't hurt that the vice president of the country at that time was Charles Curtis, who was himself of Native American descent. Templeton was designated by the U.S. government to aid in Lila Jimerson's defense and took the assignment on March 25.

Lila Jimerson pleaded not guilty to the charges of first-degree murder. She testified that she had discussed the plans with Henri and that Nancy had actually carried out the deed. Jimerson was not in the best health when the trial began, and on April 1, she collapsed in the courtroom from tuberculosis. The judge proclaimed a mistrial since there was no telling when Lila might be able to return to the court. While in her hospital bed, Lila Jimerson withdrew her plea of not guilty and pleaded guilty instead. A second trial was held in which she could have received a sentence of twenty years in prison for second-degree murder. Then, on April 22, Jimerson once more decided to change her plea back to not guilty and would stand trial once more for first-degree murder. At this point, greatly concerned that she would not receive proper counsel, the reservation elders contacted famed attorney Clarence Darrow to take the case. Darrow spoke with Lila's attorneys but in the end turned the case down because there was the chance that he might lose, and as he explained, he would not wish to endanger his client in an attempt to get a better verdict.

During the second trial, police commissioner Austin Roche testified that it was a cold, calculated murder in which he believed Mr. Marchand had no involvement. Jimerson was now on trial as an accomplice to Bowen, who had pleaded guilty to the murder itself. Jimerson's attorneys needed to prove that Nancy Bowen acted alone, but Bowen was not about to let Jimerson get away with that. Furthermore, Nancy Bowen swore that she had received letters telling her that Clotilde Marchand was a "white witch of Buffalo"

Deeper and Deeper

On the stand, Nancy Bowen told the court that she had certain evidence that her reason for killing Mrs. Marchand was justified. The spirits of dead warriors were called upon for their aid. Bowen took a search party to the Indian burial ground on the Cattaraugus reservation. She led them to the graves of warriors who had been dead for many years. With assistance from Anson Jimerson, Lila's father, searchers dug up the graves and found food and whiskey that the warriors would need in order to travel to help kill the "white witch," as well as effigies of Clotilde Marchand to help them identify her. One of these dolls made of paper was cut from a love letter sent to Lila Jimerson in what appeared to be Henri Marchand's handwriting. They further searched the Jimerson house and found another letter to Lila from Henri while he had been away in Bermuda. The last line of this letter read, "If you are as glad to see me as I am to see you when I come back it will be a real love meeting." Also found in Jimerson's home was a photograph of Henri Marchand taken in Bermuda. The letter was addressed specifically to Lila Jimerson, so there was no chance it had been intercepted on its way to his wife. Newspapers stated that Nancy Bowen also created witch medicine and had boiled a cloth effigy in it, and that set into motion the events that would kill the witch, Clotilde Marchand.

During the trial, Henri was held in the Erie County jail as a material witness. It was obvious he was under strain, and he denied any previous knowledge of the plot to kill his wife. "I'm no criminal. I lived happily with my wife for thirty-two years. Why should I want to kill her? We have never been separated. We have had a happy life together. That is all I can say." Henri's distress and a threat to commit suicide led to him being placed under heavy guard.

In the first trial, Henri Marchand was raked over the coals right along with the two Indian women as the prosecutor looked for some way to connect him to the foul deed. It came out at the trial, when Henri Marchand took the stand, that Lila Jimerson had asked for a lock of Clotilde's hair two years prior to the slaying. Henri consulted with an expert on Indian society and was told that what Lila was asking for was part of Indian sorcery and advised not to give her the hair. Henri did not. As far as Henri was concerned, this meant he had no idea that the women were practicing witchcraft, but the prosecutor used the incident to show that Henri knew they were practicing sorcery up to two years before Mrs. Marchand was killed, and Henri had said nothing about it, nor did he end his relationship with Jimerson.

Interestingly, Henri Marchand was not asked to testify in Jimerson's second trial at the end of 1931, perhaps because by then he had moved to the outskirts of Albany and was living with his new wife, an eighteen-year-old relative of his "dearly departed," Clotilde.

Nancy Bowen was found guilty and went to jail as soon as Jimerson's second trial was completed. Indians on the reservation felt that Nancy Bowen was being sacrificed because she said on the stand that she was guilty of the crime. Her lawyers decided to plead not guilty even though it could have meant a death sentence. In what may seem like an anticlimactic conclusion, because Jimerson was found innocent and Bowen was given a sentence of time served, both women were released in a little more than a year. Henri Marchand died in 1951. Lila Jimerson married and lived until 1972.

This case drew spectators from far and wide to the court and could be a thriller novel today. The crime was not spoken of in the Marchand family, and when there were grandchildren, they did not learn of it until they were adults. The Indian tribe's reputation was at stake, and the scandal could have closed the doors of the practically new museum, but it did not, for which the museum was grateful. Although most of the famed dioramas by the Marchands are no longer on display at the Buffalo Museum of Science, later works by George and Paul Marchand live on, frozen in time in the museum's Marchand Hall, an incredible colorful display of wax-sculptured plants from the Niagara Region. The museum also holds the only known collection of Paul's insect examples. The duo left the museum's employ in 1944, but Paul returned in 1965, and his expertise is what is seen today. Their father's legacy was quite different but nonetheless memorable and certainly wicked.

Hurry, Hurry, Hurry, Step Right Up!

Everyone seemed to be looking for a thrill, if only because there were thrills to be had, and one of the most thrilling places during the mid- to late 1800s was Niagara Falls, "Honeymoon Capital of the World." But of course for it to be thrilling beyond a first visit or a first night, it had to offer more than one of the world's natural wonders and a honeymoon suite. Niagara Falls offered spectacle.

Excitement over this beautiful natural wonder lives on in both the United States and Canada. Both have a shared history that dates back to man's earliest exploration of the Niagara Region. Both countries have also shared venues and rivalries for power that went beyond the beauty of the falls.

View of the eighty-foot enclosed staircase to the water. Biddle Stair, Goat Island, July 22, 1846. *Courtesy of the Library of Congress Print and Photographs Division.*

The story of the Niagara Falls Museum begins with Table Rock, a gigantic overhanging ledge of ancient rock on the precipice at Niagara Falls, Canada. Table Rock was a longtime draw for tourists year round, especially in winter, when it became coated with a glistening sheet of ice. But the geological formation is no more than a name on a sign today. It began to deteriorate with a first rock fall in 1818, and then in 1850, a carriage sitting on the precipice tumbled to its destruction when nearly one-third of the ledge crumbled. Fortunately, the driver of that carriage was not in it at the time and was spared certain death. Finally, in 1935, the Niagara Parks Commission decided to blast away the remaining section of rock to protect tourists. It was near to this overhang of rock that English-born Thomas Barnett moved in the early 1820s. He built Canada's first museum in an old brewery in 1827 and named the museum Table Rock Museum.

Barnett was an expert taxidermist, so his early displays were composed mainly of his own collection of mounted animals. It stands to reason with the region's history that this museum also housed a number of Native American artifacts. In addition, there were many objects of interest similar to those collected at any number of libraries during that period, such as shells and minerals. In that age of curiosity, however, the museum could not thrive on these exhibits alone. What made Barnett's museum famous were some of his later acquisitions.

In 1854, Thomas's son, Sydney Barnett, made his first of three visits to Egypt, returning with four mummies and many other Egyptian artifacts. In 1857, the museum acquired mastodon remains following their discovery in Ontario. An 1844, inventory listed approximately five thousand items held by the museum, and in 1859, it had grown to include the Egyptian collection, as well as a collection of eggs, ancient and modern coins and Asian relics. The Barnetts added a humpback whale skeleton in 1873. The museum acquired many objects from the 1901 Pan-American Exposition in Buffalo, New York, but by that time the museum was no longer under ownership of the Barnett family. In fact, Thomas Barnett's beloved museum was already sold in 1878. Thomas Barnett died in 1890.

The area around Table Rock is sometimes called "the Front," and in 1882, it was made into today's lovely Queen Victoria Park, which also incorporated parts of an old private estate known as Clifton Hill. Today, the Clifton Hill area is often referred to as the "Vegas of Canada," with its wax museums, haunted houses, rides, flashing lights and other distractions and attractions, but this playground for tourists may never have been born if not for Thomas Barnett and his longtime rival, Saul Davis. Searching for history on the two entrepreneurs, one might find that Barnett and Davis are like angel and demon, but both played a role in this flashy fight for attention that has become Niagara Falls, Canada.

Almost from the opening of the museum, Davis and Barnett went head to head, Davis having a competitive spirit and Barnett a deep love for his "hobby." They were not necessarily the only ones fighting for the goldmine that Niagara Falls became, with the constant flow of well-to-do tourist patrons. It's just that theirs was an antagonistic rivalry that captured the attention of legal authorities on several occasions.

In 1853, Saul Davis, who owned the Prospect House hotel, sold it to his cousin and built another hotel deliberately near Barnett's museum. He called this hotel Table Rock House. In many ways, the rivalry between the two men made Barnett's museum all the better. As a result of his fears that his "business" would not win patrons, Barnett continued his search for the most sensational items to exhibit. Davis spent an exorbitant amount of time in the shadows, whispering to Barnett's customers, waylaying them and enticing them away from the museum and into his own web of delights. The whole area of "the Front" was laden with fierce competition for business and also drew thieves, prostitutes and con artists looking for unwary tourists. Table Rock House gained the nickname "Den of Forty Thieves," and it's easy to see why.

From as early as the 1700s, courageous curiosity-seekers were climbing down the side of the gorge around Table Rock. They used roots, branches and jutting rocks, or even rope ladders, to do so. By the time Barnett opened his museum, other venues had stairways leading down to the water's edge for a spectacular close-up view of the falls from its base. Barnett went into direct competition with another hotel owner, Isaiah Starkey, and in turn, Davis went into competition with Barnett. But Davis had a no-holds-barred attitude toward business, whereas Barnett wanted to maintain a high-class museum and even purchased design plans from Europe to house his collection. Davis had no qualms about placing his workers, whom many called henchmen, on the street in view of Barnett's establishment to lure customers away. Davis and his henchmen even went so far as to offer a free trip down his stairs. His ploy? He basically charged patrons to come back up again. First, Davis "persuaded," practically forced, patrons to don raincoats to keep themselves dry, but he didn't bother to tell them they'd have to pay a fee for the raincoats when they climbed up again—and of course, the fee was high.

In 1860, Davis was granted permission to run a walking tour to the base of the Horseshoe Falls. The walking tour had previously been one of Barnett's attractions, so Davis undercut him in that respect. Saul Davis's permission required him to give free access to the falls and to charge no more than a quarter to use his stairs, but he didn't make it easy for tourists to get to the falls. He built a stone wall with a gate, locking Barnett's customers out and keeping them from going to the falls. Davis didn't make it easy for his own patrons either. During a court trial following complaints from customers, one patron testified that he was told he could have his photograph taken for fifty cents, but when he returned to collect the photo, the price had gone up to four dollars. Mysteriously, the photographer was no longer present on the job.

Davis would do anything for a buck, and it seems he would stop at nothing to outdo his competition. Signs apparently showed up on Barnett's stairs

Niagara Falls is sometimes called the "Vegas of Canada." *Courtesy of the Library of Congress Print and Photographs Division.*

saying that they were unsafe, and in yet another show of audacity, Davis sold tickets to use his stairs and told patrons that the purchase price included admission to Barnett's museum. At this, angry ticket holders reported Davis and Barnett to the police. The feud escalated, and in April 1865, Davis's stairs were burned to the ground, forcing him to use Barnett's staircase. Davis wanted free access, but of course Barnett refused. Some of Davis's henchmen began throwing rocks and other objects over the gorge rim at Barnett's customers.

In 1869, Barnett was given permission for full access to the slope behind his museum, which allowed tourists to walk to the base of the Horseshoe Falls. Saul Davis built a new stairway and began "Behind the Sheet," an attraction to enter the tunnels behind the falls. It was only a matter of time before the feud took to the streets, and when it did, someone got hurt. In fact, someone was killed.

Saul Davis's son, Edward, was walking past Barnett's museum on the evening of July 25, 1870, when a group of Barnett's workers began throwing things at him, mostly rocks and sticks. Edward, who carried a gun, was afraid for his life and shot at one of the attackers, hitting him. The man died, and Edward was arrested. However, he was acquitted, probably on the grounds of self-defense. As fate would have it, Barnett's son, Sydney, played a role in the incident that led to the shooting.

Business fell off, and Barnett was once more forced to be the entrepreneur and entertainer that had gained his museum early fame. Wild West shows were gaining popularity, and Barnett planned an extravaganza in 1872, a *Great Buffalo Hunt* to include the killing of live animals hosted by none other than the great "Wild Bill" Hickok. Barnett expected fifty thousand people in attendance, but even with his advance publicity and Hickok on the bill, only three thousand people showed. To make matters worse, many of the animals had gotten sick and died before the show began. "Buffalo Bill" Cody, not Hickok, was to have been his headliner for the *Buffalo Hunt*, but the government would not allow Indians to leave the reservation to participate.

Thomas Barnett lost money on the show and could not pay his debts. His museum was doomed. In an epic twist of fate, Barnett's museum went bankrupt in 1877, and it was Saul Davis who bought it and its contents. So Davis gained Barnett's tour business and his museum. One can only imagine how Thomas Barnett must have mourned the loss.

But the museum's woes did not end when Davis bought it. The Niagara Parks Commission was formed in 1882 and decided to make the area that encompassed the Front into Queen Victoria Park. At this time, Davis was forced to move the museum across the river to Niagara Falls, New York, and over the next few years, he acquired additional mummies and exchanged artifacts with P.T. Barnum. Yet more misfortunes for the museum were forthcoming. The museum had a living or zoological display, but complaints of bad smells and loud noises forced that section to be closed in 1892. Eventually, in 1942, Davis's family sold the museum to Jacob Sherman, but in 1958, the same thing happened to him that had happened to Davis in Canada. New York State decided to extend its park system, and the museum had to move back to Canada, where it was housed in an old corset factory. In 1999, the Sherman family closed the museum and sold the collection to a private collector, William Jamieson of Toronto. The only things they kept for posterity, which are now housed in another museum, were the daredevil and local artifacts.

Could it be that the museum was suffering from some sort of curse that drove men to possess it, lose it, close it or have to move it? If you believe in

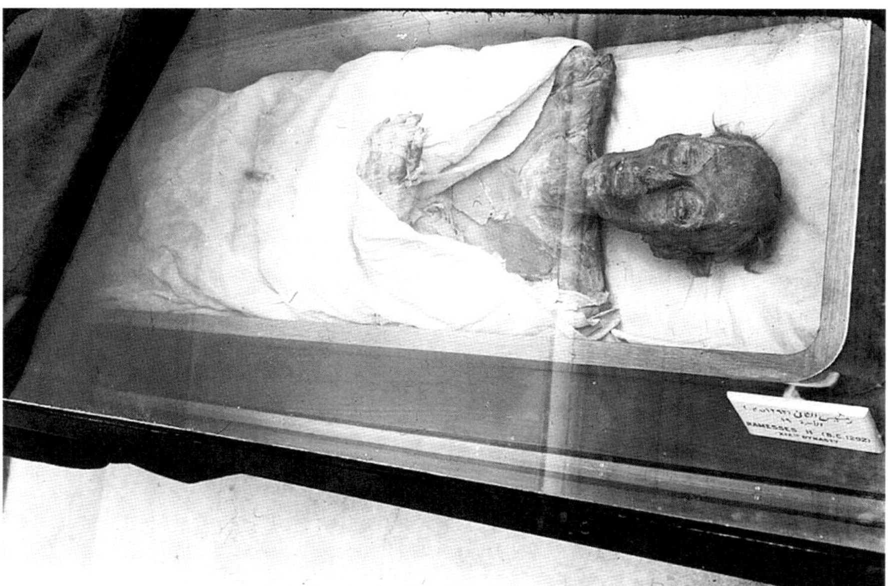

Viewed as curiosities, many Egyptian artifacts ended up in sideshow venues. *Courtesy of the Library of Congress Print and Photographs Division.*

such curses as the curse of the mummy, perhaps that is one explanation. You see, during all those years that the museum was open, at least until William Jamieson sold off a few of the artifacts, including the Egyptian collection, a great treasure lay right under their noses. A patron visiting the collection had taken notice of one mummy in particular. He was struck by the manner with which it had been preserved and how its arms were crossed. This led him to research and exploration that brought him back to the collection sometime later. As it turned out, that mummy purchased in Egypt by Sydney Barnett over one hundred years earlier was one of Egypt's greatest kings. DNA testing found it to be none other than Ramesses I, founding pharaoh of Egypt's nineteenth dynasty, father to Seti I and grandfather to Ramesses II, who brought Egypt to a new height.

After lying dusty in Niagara Falls, being viewed by curiosity-seeking tourists and perhaps laughed at by small children, the pharaoh was returned to Egypt with ceremony in 2003. Oh, what would Thomas Barnett and Saul Davis have done had they known that this great king was in their possession? We will never know, but the imagination can attach itself to history and conjure a "Vegas of Canada" with pyramids, camels and a great sphinx.

Many changes and improvements came to the attractions over the years. A hydraulic lift took the place of the infamous stairs in 1889, and Table Rock House was demolished in 1925 after falling into disrepair. A new building and road were constructed. This is the site of the tours today. The "Behind the Sheet" or "Scenic Tunnels" tour began there and is today called "Journey Behind the Falls." Niagara Falls still attracts millions of visitors to the region from all over the world. Tourists walk on the very place where Barnett dreamed of a great museum and Davis dreamed of a great fortune, yet sadly this tale is largely forgotten in the lights, sights, smells and sounds of modern Niagara Falls, Canada. Some still call Thomas Barnett the "Museum Man."

Selected Bibliography

Parker, Arthur C. *Skunny Wundy: Seneca Indian Tale.* Syracuse, NY: Syracuse University Press, 1994.

Rapp, Marvin A. *Canal Water and Whiskey*. Buffalo, NY: Heritage Press, 1992.

Vogel, Michael. *America's Crossroads: Buffalo's Canal Street/Dante Place.* Buffalo, NY: Heritage Press, 1993.

Internet Resources

American Mafia. www.onewal.com.

Apalachin, New York. www.apalachin.net.

Buffalo Architecture and History. www.buffaloah.com.

Buffalo Courier Express Library. www.library.buffalostate.edu.

Buffalo Museum of Science. www.sciencebuff.org.

Buffalo News. www.buffalonews.com.

Buffalo Spree Magazine. www.buffalospreemagazine.com.

Buffalonian. www.buffalonian.com.

Early Canada History Narratives. www.uppercanadahistory.ca.

Egyptian Museum. www.egyptianmuseum.com.

Erie Canal Harbor Development Corp. www.eriecanalharbor.com.

Erie Canal History. www.eriecanalhistory.com.

Essortment. www.essortment.com.

Federal Bureau of Investigation. www.fbi.gov.
Free Essays, Cliff Notes and Term Paper Database. www.essays.cc.
Laborers for Justice and the Laborers Network. www.thelaborers.net.
La Cosa Nostra Database. www.lacndb.com.
Newspaper Abstracts: Erie County. www.newspaperabstracts.com.
Niagara Falls Thunder Alley. www.niagarafrontier.com.
Niagara Museum. www.niagaramuseum.com.
Niagara Times. www.niagaratimes.com.
Official Lockport, NY Government and Tourism Information. www.elockport.com.
155th New York Volunteer Infantry Reenactment Regiment. www.acsu.buffalo.edu/~dbertuca/g/FenianRaid.html.
Post-Gazette. www.post-gazette.com.
Rick Porrello's American Mafia. www.americanmafia.com.
State University of New York at Oswego. www.oswego.edu.
Time. www.time.com.
Ulrichs Tavern. www.ulrichstavern.net.
University at Buffalo Libraries. www.library.buffalo.edu.
Wikipedia, the free encyclopedia. www.wikipedia.org.
Wikisource. www.wikisource.org.
Your Dictionary. www.biography.yourdictionary.com.

OTHER SOURCES

Buffalo Erie County Historical Society. www.bechs.org.
David Rumsey Map Collection. www.davidrumsey.com.
Fort Niagara. www.oldfortniagara.org. (716-745-7611)
Shaun O'Boyle: Portraits of Place, Modern Ruins Photographs. www.oboylephoto.com.
U.S. History Images. www.ushistoryimages.com.

About the Author

Carrying a pocketful of stories, Lorna MacDonald Czarnota has been entertaining, teaching and reaching audiences of all ages since 1985. She has traveled throughout the United States, Canada and Ireland. Lorna specializes in original tales, adaptation of classic fairy tales (often with music) and Celtic, historical and healing stories. Her historical presentations include colonial America, medieval times, the American Civil War and the Dust Bowl era. Lorna sang Depression-era songs with the Blue Eagle String Band.

Lorna is the author of *Legends, Lore and Secrets of Western New York*, *Medieval Tales that Kids Can Read and Tell*, "One Lace Glove," *August House Book of Scary Stories*, "The Bleeding Heart" and *The Healing Heart Community.*